Cool Devotions For Gu

AGES 10-12

GOTTA HAVE GOD 3

ROSEKiDZ

An imprint of Rose Publishing, Inc.
Carson, CA
www.Rose-Publishing.com

FAMILY BOOK DEDICATION:

For Rachel, Bethany, and Kevin for raising such outstanding parents!
—H.M.B. and J.F.N.B.

GOTTA HAVE GOD VOLUME 3 FOR AGES 10-12
©2014 by H. Michael Brewer and Janet Neff Brewer, fifth printing
ISBN 10: 1-58411-098-8
ISBN 13: 978-1-58411-098-9
RoseKidz reorder#: LP46969

Juvenile Nonfiction / Religion / Devotion & Prayer

RoseKidz
An imprint of Rose Publishing, Inc.
17909 Adria Maru Lane
Carson, CA 90746
www.Rose-Publishing.com

Cover Illustrator: Dave Carleson
Interior Illustrator: Brie Spangler

Printed in South Korea

Cool Devotions For Guys

GOTTA
HAVE
GOD 3

AGES 10-12

H. MICHAEL BREWER
AND JANET NEFF BREWER

TABLE OF CONTENTS

INTRODUCTION

THIS BOOK IS ABOUT GETTING TO KNOW GOD, getting to know ourselves, and having fun. Anybody got a problem with having fun while we learn about God?

You, there. The guy in the back. Put your hand down. There's a reason why God and fun each have three letters. They go together! Now get with the program.

Let's see... Where were we? Oh, yeah. We're going to have fun reading stories, studying the Bible, and doing awesome activities. There are answers at the end of the book, but you probably won't need them. You look pretty smart.

You in the back again... You have a question? Should you start on page one and read straight through? Nah, you can read these stories in any order. Start at the back if you want to. Some of the stories fit together to make a bigger story, but each one will make sense by itself.

Another question? What kind of batteries does this book use? No batteries. This book is hand-powered. But you will need a pencil, and having a Bible would be great.

Sigh... Kid in the back, this is the last question I'm answering. Do we grade this book on the curve? No grades! No tests! No report cards! Remember the part about having fun? Sheesh.

Okay, you've spent enough time on this Introduction.

TURN THE PAGE.
GET STARTED ALREADY.
AND HAVE FUN!

CHAPTER ONE

GETTING TO KNOW GOD

GOD OF THE UNIVERSE
God made everything.
He counts the stars and calls them all by name.- Psalm 147:4

A BIG, BIG GOD

Mr. Wylie said, "Today's lesson is astronomy."

A picture of the Earth appeared on the classroom screen, shining like a jewel in outer space.

"Planet Earth," Mr. Wylie said. "Has anybody visited there?"

Tyler chuckled. He loved science class.

"It's a big place," Mr. Wylie continued. "If we could find a bathroom scale big enough to lay the planet on we would find that Earth weighs over six billion trillion tons. That's a six followed by twenty-one zeroes. Even if you missed every question on every test, you couldn't get that many zeroes."

Tyler heard more laughter and a few groans.

"Of course, the Earth is just one planet of eight circling the sun," Mr. Wylie told the class. "There used to be nine planets before poor Pluto was kicked out of the planet club."

The screen showed a cartoon planet with arms and legs. He held a sign that said, "I am too a planet!"

Mr. Wylie pretended to wipe away a tear. "The sun is a star big enough to swallow one million Earths," he said.

"I hope it doesn't get hungry," said a boy in the back.

"And in our galaxy, there are roughly one hundred billion stars," Mr. Wylie said as the Milky Way flashed on the screen.

"Are there other galaxies?" asked a girl near Tyler.

"Absolutely," said Mr. Wylie. "Using our best telescopes, our scientists can spot billions of galaxies, and there are many more that we can't see."

Mr. Wylie paused and turned to the class.

"In other words," the teacher said, "it's a big, big universe."

"And a big, big God," Tyler whispered.

YOUR TURN

1. Of all the animals God has made, which is your favorite? What about your favorite weather?

PRAYER God, You are totally amazing. I can't even imagine all the things You have made. Thanks for making me, too. Amen.

THE CREATOR

Yeah, God made *everything*. Can you believe it? The very first chapter of the Bible tells about God creating the world. We've told the story here, but a few of the words are wrong. All you have to do is replace the wrong words with the right words. To make it really easy, the right word will always rhyme with the long herd. Uh, I mean wrong word. Okay, you know what I'm trying to say. Get to work!

On the first day, God made kite. And it was good. _____

On the second day, God made the pie. And it was amazing. _____

On the third day, God made the band and the key. And it was terrific. _____ and _____

On the fourth day, God made the bun, goon, and cars. And it was excellent. _____, _____, and _____

On the fifth day, God made dishes and words. And it was wonderful. _____ and _____

On the sixth day, God made logs, hats, and all kinds of animals that give us companionship today. God also made steeple. And it was awesome. _____, _____, and _____

On the seventh day, God nested. _____

GOD IS EVERYWHERE

God is everywhere, all the time.

"Do not I fill heaven and earth?"
declares the Lord.

– Jeremiah 23:24

THE COOKIE TRAY

Randy and Travis were in the lunch line at Camp Red Lake. Randy pointed at a bowl of cookies near the end of the line. Next to the tray was a hand-written sign that read: "One Cookie Per Camper. God Is Watching!"

Randy said, "That's funny," as he took a chocolate chip cookie.

Travis picked out an oatmeal cookie and said, "It creeps me out. If God is everywhere, He sees everything I do."

Randy shrugged as they settled at a table. "So?"

Travis lowered his voice. "God saw me when I put toothpaste in Counselor Stan's sock."

"That was you?" Randy said.

"Shhh!" Travis said. "And I put sugar in the salt shaker at table seven. Do you think God is trying to catch me doing stuff?"

"God isn't like a principal in the sky trying to punish us," Randy said.

"But God's everywhere!" Travis said.

"Yeah, like at the pool yesterday when you did that crazy dive," Randy said.

"The life guard made me sit out the rest of pool time," Travis grumped.

"Your head barely missed the diving board," he said. "You could have been hurt."

"But I wasn't," Travis said.

"Maybe because God was keeping an eye on you," Randy said. "After all, He saw the dive. Maybe He kept you from konking your head."

"Do you think so?" Travis asked.

"Sure," Randy said. "God isn't just watching us, He is watching over us."

The camp cook came from the kitchen. "We have extra cookies if anyone wants seconds," he called.

"Wow!" Travis said. "God really is watching over us."

YOUR TURN

1. Does it make you feel good or bad that God is always with you? Why do you feel that way?

_____

PRAYER   God, I like to keep on the move. Thanks for keeping up with me no matter where I go or what I'm doing. Amen.

HERE, THERE, AND EVERYWHERE!

God is with us no matter where we go. Here are some places near and far that you could go and God would still be with you. Fill in the blanks, using the clues after each sentence. You might also need to look up the verse in the Bible that contains the word you need.

GOD IS WITH ME IN THE DARKEST _____
Clue #1 - This is a place where it's always cool.
Clue #2 – Joshua 10:16

GOD IS WITH ME ABOVE THE _____
Clue #1 – You'd better wear a rain coat and a parachute.
Clue #2 – Psalm 68:4

GOD IS WITH ME IF I FLY TO THE _____
Clue #1 - This is a place very few men—and no women—have visited.
Clue #2 – Psalm 89:37

GOD IS WITH ME IN A _____
Clue #1 – I hope your kite
            doesn't end up here.
Clue #2 – 1 Samuel 10:3

GOD IS WITH ME IN THE _____
Clue #1 - This is a wild and lonely place.
Clue #2 – Isaiah 35:6

GOD IS WITH ME ON A _____
Clue #1 – There might be snow on top.
Clue #2 – Ezekiel 17:22

GOD IS WITH ME ON THE
_____
Clue #1 – This place is fishy.
Clue #2 – Job 9:8

GOD OUR HELPER

God helps us.
God is our refuge and strength,
an ever-present help in trouble.
– Psalm 46:1

THE LOST BOOK

"That book has to be here," Braden said. He and Ned studied the piles of clothing, comic books, and toys that filled his bedroom.

"If I can't find it, I'll have to pay the library seventeen bucks," Braden complained.

Ned shook his head and said, "You could lose a school bus in this mess."

"That's a big help," Braden said.

"You go to church," Ned said. "Maybe God will show you where your book is."

Braden frowned. He didn't like it when Ned made fun of his church.

"You told me God likes to help people," Ned continued. "Why isn't he helping me now?"

Braden thought, God is helping me not lose my temper. He said, "I don't think it works that way."

"Why not?" Ned asked.

"How would you feel if your mom came to school and fed you your lunch?" Braden asked.

"I'd hide under the table," Ned said.

"What if your dad showed up at practice to tie your shoes?"

"I'd feel stupid if I couldn't do that stuff for myself," Ned said.

"Exactly," said Braden. "Growing up means learning to do things on our own. If God found every lost book, gave me every test answer, and helped me hit every baseball, I'd never learn anything."

"So God's not going to help you look for your library book?" Ned asked.

Now it was Braden's turn to smile.

"Maybe God sent you to help me look," he said. "Now get to work."

"Okay," Ned said with a sigh. "You crawl under the bed and I'll check the closet. What's the name of the book?"

"The title is How To Get Organized," Braden said.

YOUR TURN

1. Sometimes we don't get what we ask for in prayer. Why is this?

_____

 **PRAYER** God, sometimes I need Your help. Other times it's better for me to do it myself, even if I mess up. Whenever I ask for Your help, I trust You to do what's best for me. Amen.

WHAT A HELPER!

God helps us in so many ways. Here's a list of some of the ways God reaches into our lives to give us help. Some of the words go from down to up, some are backwards, and some are diagonal.

FAMILY	PROTECTION
COMFORT	COURAGE
GUIDANCE	HEALING
PEACE	LOVE
PATIENCE	FRIENDS

```
S  P  G  N  I  L  A  E  H  U  I  E
C  A  R  Q  E  D  S  H  F  P  O  G
O  M  R  J  T  U  E  H  N  Q  W  J
U  M  P  J  C  O  M  F  O  R  T  I
R  W  A  Q  P  S  I  T  I  S  L  Y
A  D  T  H  G  D  W  P  T  N  M  L
G  U  I  D  A  N  C  E  C  O  F  I
E  M  E  B  A  E  E  A  E  Y  E  M
N  D  N  V  I  I  J  C  T  V  D  A
L  F  C  K  F  R  U  E  O  S  A  F
D  H  E  I  E  F  W  L  R  P  D  I
B  X  Z  H  G  D  P  F  P  W  T  A
```

GOD OUR PROTECTOR

God always answers our prayers, but sometimes the answer is no.

I have loved you with an everlasting love.
– Jeremiah 31:3

CHOCOLATE DANGER

Drake sat on the floor, staring at Charles with pleading brown eyes. Charles nibbled the brownie and said, "No, Drake. No people food for dogs."

Drake whined, watching every bite that entered Charles' mouth.

Charles shook his head.

"Drake, remember that time you got into my plate when I left the room for a minute? You gobbled down meatballs in curry sauce? You threw up and felt awful."

Charles reached into his pocket and took out a doggy treat.

"Here's a chewie stick," Charles said.

He held it out to Drake, who took it from his hand, and hid the treat under the sofa. He returned to sit near Charles, again staring at the brownie.

"Chocolate is bad for dogs," Charles said. "I love you too much to give you this brownie. You don't know what's good for you."

Charles took another bite and washed it down with milk.

"I don't always get what I want, either," Charles told Drake. "Sometimes I pray so hard for something, and God doesn't give it to me. That doesn't mean God doesn't love me. God knows what will be good for me and what won't, so I trust Him to decide. God loves me too much to give me things that would be bad for me."

He finished the brownie and scooped Drake onto his lap.

"Just like I love you, scruffy dog."

The puppy rolled on his back and held his paws in the air. Charles rubbed his belly and Drake wiggled in pleasure.

"A belly rub is better than a brownie," Charles said, putting his face close to Drake's. The dog licked Charles on the nose and wagged his tail.

1. Have you ever asked God for something you didn't get?

_____

God, thanks for saying no sometimes. I know You do that because You want what's best for me. Amen.

YES OR NO?

Sometimes we can't figure out why God doesn't give us what we ask for, but we know that God always treats us with love. Here are some prayers that God didn't say YES to. Can you fill in reasons why God might have said NO?

Aiden prayed for God to make him captain of the football team.

_____

Jeff prayed for an A on his Social Studies test. Then he played computer games instead of studying.

_____

Dean prayed for a motorized dirt bike.

_____

Jacob prayed for his grandfather to change his mind and let him drive the four-wheeler on his farm.

_____

While walking to the store, Drew prayed to find enough money to buy a comic book.

_____

Jesse prayed that his parents wouldn't find out about the R-rated movie he watched at his friend's house.

GOD IS FOREVER
God is always the same.
The Father...does not change like shifting shadows.
– James 1:17

THE VOCABULARY TEST

Bryce frowned at his weekly list of vocabulary words. What a waste of time. These were words nobody would ever use. Maybe on a quiz show somebody might win a million dollars with one of these words, but you'd never hear any of these words in real life.

Like "immutable." He glanced at the meaning of the word: "Never changing. Always the same."

How was he supposed to use that in a sentence? "The Earth is immutable." Not true. The Earth is changing all the time. Even the continents are slowly drifting. "The sky is immutable." Wrong again. What was that stuff thinning out in the sky? Ozone?

He tried to think of something that lasts a long time. Maybe the sun? Nah, that wouldn't work. Stars might shine for billions of years, but eventually they burn out. Everything changes. Nothing lasts. There's nothing you can count on in this world.

He started getting angry about "immutable." Why would somebody invent a word that cannot be used?

He could imagine that goofy girl in English class saying, "Love lasts forever. Love is immutable."

Barf! That was fine for movies and TV shows, but not in the real world. His Mom and Dad had stopped loving each other. Now they were divorced and living in different houses. Love is not immutable, Bryce decided. Neither are families.

Then he remembered something his pastor had said at church: God's love for us never changes. It's always been there, and it will be there forever, even after all the stars in the universe burn out. Bryce smiled and thought to himself, "God's love is immutable."

YOUR TURN

1. Does God ever change? Explain your thinking.

God, I can always count on You. You're always on my side, and nothing could ever make You stop loving me. Everything else in the world might change, but not You. Not now. Not ever. Amen.

IMMUTABLE

Good will never change his mind about loving you and me. He will never take back his guarantee to have a place for us in heaven. He will never break a promise. Here is something from Psalm 102 that you can say to God.

To break the code, cross out every P and B and C. Then change every X to E. Change every Z to Y. And change every Q to R. When you've figured out the message, write it in the word balloon as a prayer to God.

Zbocpu qxmcpabin tpchx sapcbmx, abcnd
zobcuq zxacqs wbiclpl nxpcbvxq xncbpd.

GOD NEVER FORGETS US
God knows everything.

For God is greater than our hearts, and he knows everything.
– I John 3:20

WHAT'S YOUR NAME?

Principal Robeson dropped into class to talk about the new Spanish Club.

"Does anyone have questions?" the principal asked.

Connor raised his hand to find out when the club would have its first meeting. The principal saw him and said, "Yes, young man in the back row?"

After class, on the way to math, Connor said to his friend Tim, "Our principal doesn't know my name. I've been in this school for three years. I run cross country, and I'm President of the Chess Club."

"I don't think he knows anybody's name," Tim said.

"I've been a student helper in the office for two years," Connor said. "He sees me every day and still doesn't know who I am! It's like I'm nobody."

"I know your name," said Tim.

Connor grinned at his friend and said, "But you're just another nobody."

"God knows your name, and he's somebody," Tim said. "God is more important than Principal Robeson."

Connor laughed.

"Way more important," he said.

"And God has more people to watch over than our Principal," Tim added.

"Way more people," Connor agreed, "along with animals and plants and maybe even people on other planets."

"But even though He's taking care of everyone and everything in the whole world, God knows your name," Tim said.

"Not just my name," Connor said. "He knows my grade point average, my shoe size, and my favorite drinking fountain."

"You have a favorite drinking fountain?" Tim asked.

"Sure," Connor said.

"I didn't know that," Tim said.

"But God knows it," Connor said. "That proves God knows more than you do."

"Way more," Tim said. "Way, way more."

YOUR TURN

1. When people forget your name, how does it make you feel?

_____

PRAYER God, I never see my name in the newspaper or my face on TV, but I know I'm important to You. That makes me feel great! Amen.

GOD ONLY KNOWS

od knows you inside and out, every single thing. Crack the code to see some of the things God knows about you. What other things can you think of that God knows about you?

Things that %?*^&[$ < you
_____

Things that make you &!\\\~
_____

Your ^>!+{
_____

Your {/##${{${
_____

Your {$ #?$ [{
_____

How many &!*?{ !?$ ><
~>/? &$!8
_____

! = A	$ = E	* = I	\ = P	
@ = B	% = F	+ = L	? = R	/ = U
# = C	^ = G	< = N	{ = S	~ = Y
8 = D	& = H	> = O	[= T	

GOD NEVER GIVES UP

God is patient.

The Lord is not slow in keeping his promise, as some understand slowness. He is patient with you, not wanting anyone to perish, but everyone to come to repentance.
– Isaiah 26:4

THE EAR KILLER

Aaaarroooaaahhh!

Max covered his ears with his hands. "What is that horrible sound?"

Austin looked up from his math book. He and Max were working on homework in Austin's room.

"It's my little sister Hayley, practicing her trumpet," Austin said. "She's only been taking lessons about a month."

"It's scrambling my brain," Max said. "Like an elephant being tortured."

"Or a dump truck running over garbage cans," Austin suggested.

"Or an angry cat fighting with a bagpipe," Max said.

"She'll get better with practice. Someday she'll sound great," said Austin.

"How can you be so patient?" Max asked.

Austin thought about it for a moment. "Remember how I used to be late for Sunday School?" he asked.

"Sure," Max said. "You live next door to the church, but you could never get there on time."

"I'd show up ten minutes late still buttoning my shirt," Austin laughed. "And Mr. Dent would just smile. He'd say, 'God is patient with me, and I can be patient with you. Maybe you'll make it next week.'"

"Now you're on time every Sunday," Max said.

"Yeah, but I was late for months, and Mr. Dent kept smiling," Austin said.

"I get it," Max said. "God is patient with you and me when we're trying to get it right, so we should be patient with others, too."

Hayley's trombone sounded like a train crashing into a glass bottle factory.

"Maybe we should be patient at my house for a while," Max suggested.

Austin folded his homework paper into his math book and stood up.

"I think that's a great idea," he said.

YOUR TURN

1. When you mess up even though you are trying to do your best, how do you think God feels about you?

PRAYER   God, I know I don't always do things that please You. Thanks for being patient and never giving up on me. Amen.

PRACTICING PATIENCE

To figure out this message from the Bile, you'll have to patiently solve the secret code. Take each letter that is blue and move it forward two places in the alphabet. For example, P becomes R.

Then take each letter that is red and move backward two spaces in the alphabet. So N becomes L.

DC RCRGGLV YKRF GXCPWQPC

(from Thessalonians 5:14)

■ BiGGER THAN THE WORLD ■
God has no limits.

But will God really dwell on earth? The heavens, even the highest heaven, cannot contain you.

– I Kings 8:27

THE RIDDLE GAME

Mason and his dad settled into their seats on the plane.

"This is a big plane," Mason said.

"This plane will carry four hundred passengers," his dad said.

"I know something that holds more," Mason said.

"A cruise ship might hold two or three thousand people," his dad said.

"I'm thinking of something that holds a lot more than that."

The plane roared down the field and rose into the air.

Mason's dad looked out the window and said, "New York City holds eight million people."

Mason said, "Come on, Dad."

His dad said, "Okay. My answer is the universe. Nothing can hold more than the universe. " He smiled in triumph. "Top that, smart guy."

"Something that holds more than the universe?" Mason asked. He pointed a finger at himself. "My answer is me."

His dad's eyebrows went up. "Prove it."

"God has no limits, right?" Mason asked. "Even the whole universe isn't big enough to hold God."

"Right," his dad agreed.

"But the Bible says God lives in me," Mason said. "That means there's room inside me for the biggest thing of all."

Mason's dad laid his head back on the neck cushion and laughed loudly. "I should never play the riddle game with you."

As a flight attendant passed, Mason's dad said, "Would you bring my son a soft drink, please? And make it a big one. This boy can hold a lot."

1. God is so big that nothing can hold Him. How would you explain this idea to a friend?

_____

PRAYER God, there is nothing that can hold You or stop You. That means I can always trust You to take care of me. Thanks for being so big! Amen.

HOUSE CLEANING

If God were coming to live in your house, you'd probably wash the windows, run the sweeper, and get out the good dishes. What if God were coming to live in you? Here's the big news: God is already living in you. What can you do to make sure that you are a good place for God to live? Here are some ideas. Draw a square around the ones you already are doing. Draw a triangle around the ones you would like to do. In the extra space at the bottom, can you add other ideas?

Be Kind To Others

Eat Healthy Food

Pray Everyday

Build Up My Mind With Learning

Tell The Truth

Worship God

Take Care of My Teeth

Practice Forgiveness

Read The Bible

Be Generous

Be Careful About Gaining Weight

Make Sure My Talking Is Clean

Treat my body with respect

GOD IS FAIR

God cares about right and wrong.

Righteousness and justice are the foundation of your throne.
– Psalm 89:14

FREE THROWS

"We lost the game by one stupid point!" Aaron said, stuffing his uniform in a gym bag.

"We're not going to the finals," Greg said.

The boys left the locker room and stepped into the cool night air.

"It's my fault," Aaron said. "I missed two free throws. If I'd sunk those baskets, we'd have won."

"Everybody misses sometimes," Greg sympathized.

"But I was praying so hard!" Aaron insisted. "I thought God was supposed to help us when we pray, but He wasn't listening tonight. How hard could it be for God to nudge a basketball through the hoop?"

Greg said, "Wouldn't that be cheating?"

"What do you mean?" Aaron asked.

"They were your free throws," Greg said. "Would it be okay for Coach to shoot them for you?"

"That's against the rules!" Aaron said.

"When Coach prays with us, He asks God to keep everyone safe and to give us a good game," Greg said. "He doesn't ask God to help us kick the other team's backside."

"I see what you mean," Aaron said. "God loves both teams. It wouldn't be fair for God to help one team win and make the other lose."

"It's a game," Greg said. "It's about how hard we practice and how well we play."

"So I guess it's not God's fault we lost," Aaron said.

"No," Greg said. "It's your fault."

"Hey!" Aaron said. "What about that shot you missed in the third quarter?"

"Nope," Greg said. "It's your fault. You said so yourself."

Laughing together, the boys ran the rest of the way home.

YOUR TURN

1. It's always good to pray, but sometimes people ask for the wrong things. Can you think of some things we shouldn't ask from God?

_____

 God, I'm glad You are fair and just. I want You to be the God of everybody, not just my God. Amen.

GOD'S JUSTICE

God is fair and God wants us to be fair, too. In each of the sentences below, underline any part that you think seems unfair or seems like something God would not want us to do. Then, try re-writing each sentence to make it describe the way God wants us to treat one another.

■ Cory slipped and fell in the mud. Then Cory tripped Mack and made him fall in the mud, too.

_____

_____

■ Brandon's sister had to stay home with Brandon while his parents went out to dinner. Brandon's sister said he was not allowed to ask a friend over to play because she didn't get to go out with her friends.

_____

_____

■ On the way to school, Aidan told Zach about his great idea for a science project. When Aidan went to tell the teacher his plans for the project, she said he'd have to find another project because Zach had just told her about his plans to do the exact same thing.

_____

_____

_____

■ Dylan ate all of his cookies and the
saved from last night's dinner. Dylan

_____

_____

_____

_____

_____

GOD'S SPECIAL NAME
God is holy.

Holy, holy, holy is the LORD Almighty;
the whole earth is full of his glory.

– Isaiah 6:3

KITCHEN TALK

Corbin's mom pulled out a chair at the kitchen table and motioned for Corbin to sit.

Oh, no, Corbin thought. *A kitchen talk.*

"What have I done now?" he asked.

"I've heard some of your friends using God's name," his mom said.

"Is that bad?" Corbin asked.

"It's fine when we're praying or talking about God," his mom said. "But it's a bad habit when people use His name disrespectfully. God is holy."

"Does that mean God is special?" Corbin asked.

"Very special," his mom said, "and that includes God's name. Think about it this way. You have play clothes you can wear when you play ball. If they get dirty or torn, it's no big deal."

Corbin remembered the day he slid into third base and ripped the back pocket from his jeans. His mom laughed and sewed the pocket back on.

"You also have dress-up clothes for special occasions," she said.

"The clothes I wear to church," Corbin said.

"Right," his mom said. "Would you grease your bike in your dress-up clothes? Or paint one of your models?"

"No way," Corbin said. "Those clothes are too special for dirty work."

"And God is too special—too holy—for us to throw His name around just to sound cool or impress people."

Corbin said, "My friends do that a lot."

His mom said, "They probably don't even know what they are doing, but I want to make sure you don't pick up that habit."

"Okay," he said.

Corbin knew that God is the most special one of all, but he decided his mom was pretty special, too.

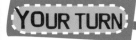

1. How would you feel if someone misused your name?

_____

God, I hope all my words and thoughts will show that You are holy and special to me. Amen.

GOING TO CHURCH

One of the ways we respect God's holiness is by worshipping Him. During worship, there are many ways to show how special God is to us. Take a look at the list below. For each action that honors the holiness of God, wright YES beside the sentence. If that behavior doesn't honor God, write NO.

Have you seen people do some of these things (or not do them) in church?

GOD OF LOVE

God is love.
*And so we know and rely on the love God
has for us. God is love.* — I John 4:16

VOLCANOES AND VALENTINES

As John and Ethan waited for the school bus, their breath made white clouds in the cold air.

"Did you hear about that earthquake in China?" Ethan asked.

"All those people killed or buried alive," John said

"You go to church, right?" Ethan asked John. "If God loves everybody, why do terrible things happen?"

"A lot of bad stuff is people hurting each other," John said.

"I get that," Ethan agreed. "But what about earthquakes, volcanoes, cancer, all the things that just happen?"

"Maybe it's to make us stronger or teach us to help each other," John said. "But I don't really know."

Ethan rubbed his cold hands together.

"You Christians look at the good things in the world, and you decide God loves us," Ethan said. "What if I look at the bad things and decide God doesn't love us?"

"I can't answer all your questions," John said. "But I know God loves us."

"How do you know?" Ethan insisted.

"God sent his son Jesus to be with us," John said. "When Jesus got here, some people made fun of Him, tortured Him, and then killed Him on a cross."

John turned to Ethan.

"Would you send your little brother to go through all of that?" John asked.

"No way," Ethan said. "I couldn't stand to see that happen to Timmy."

"Imagine how much it hurt God to see how Jesus was treated," John continued, "but God was willing to go through that pain for us."

Ethan gave it some thought.

"So in spite of the bad stuff that happens," he said, "the fact that Jesus lived and died proves God's love."

John agreed, saying. "Jesus is God's I-love-you Valentine to the whole world."

YOUR TURN

1. Does God care about people caught in earthquakes and hurricanes?

_____

 **PRAYER**   God, someday You can explain to me why so much bad stuff happens. For now, I know You love me and that's all I need to know. Amen.

GOD IS LOVE, SO IS JESUS

Everything Jesus did shows how much God loves us. Unscramble the words on the top, then match them to the correct sentences about Jesus.

LYNOLE
NYUGRH
LREDHINC
NRSNSIE
EIFL
KICS
DYYBEREVO
NBDLI

Jesus gave sight to the _____

Jesus fed the _____

Jesus healed the _____

Jesus forgave _____

Jesus made friends with the _____

Jesus played with _____

Jesus brought the dead back to _____

Jesus loved _____

Love,
God

CHAPTER TWO

THE BEST BOOK IN THE WORLD

THE ABC BOYS
The Bible is God's gift to show us how to live.
Your word is a lamp to my feet and a light for my path.
– Psalm 119:105

LISTENING FEET

Daniel climbed through the door into the tree house that the ABC boys used for their weekly meetings.

"Last as usual," Carlos said, laughing.

"Let's open the meeting," said Jacob, the ABC president.

The boys settled into a circle.

"Who are we?" Jacob asked.

"We are the Amazing Bible Club," the boys answered, their voices blending together.

"What is our only rule?" Jacob continued.

"We will try to read the Bible every day," the boys said.

Jacob nodded and said, "I'll lead the prayer." As the others bowed their heads, he said, "God, thanks for giving us the Bible so we can learn about you and how you want us to live. There are lots of good books, but the Bible is the most amazing of all. The Bible is a lamp for our feet. Amen."

"I've heard that before," Carlos said, "about the Bible being a lamp for our feet. What does that mean?"

Jacob said, "Imagine you are in a forest at midnight."

"I'd want a flashlight so I could see where I was going," Carlos said.

"Yeah," the other boys agreed.

"The Bible is our flashlight in life," Jacob explained. "In the Bible God shows us the path to walk on to keep safe."

"I get it," Carlos said. "Bible teaching like 'don't steal' keeps us out of trouble, just the way a flashlight in the dark keeps us from getting hurt."

"Cool," Mason said. "From now on, when I read the Bible, I'm not just going to listen with my head. I'm going to make sure my feet are paying attention, too!"

YOUR TURN

1. Some people say, "The Bible only works when it is open." What do you think that means?

_____

_____

PRAYER God, when I read the Bible help me hear what You are saying to me. Amen.

NEVER LOST

Most mazes are supposed to be tricky, but here is a maze that works differently. This is called a labyrinth. Once you enter the labyrinth, you cannot get lost. As long as you keep going, you will always end up in the middle. Try out the labyrinth and see.

The labyrinth is like reading the Bible. As long as we keep following God's word, we cannot get lost. He keeps us on the right path.

GOOD THINGS, GOOD BOOK

The more time we spend with the Bible, the more good things we find.

Every word of God is flawless; he is a shield to those who take refuge in him.

– Proverbs 30:5

BIBLICAL PURSUITS

"It's sharing time," Jacob announced to the Amazing Bible Club. "We read the Bible every day, and when we get together, we talk about what we've learned."

"Me first," Daniel called. "I found some great things this week." He cleared his throat and asked, "What is the longest chapter in the whole Bible?"

After a moment of silence, he added, "It's almost the next door neighbor of the shortest chapter in the Bible."

The ABC boys looked at one another, shrugging and scratching their heads. "Psalm 119 is the longest chapter in the Bible. It has 176 verses," Daniel told the club. "And the shortest chapter is Psalm 117 with only two verses."

"I'll memorize Psalm 117," Mason said to Daniel, "if you'll memorize Psalm 119."

"I've got another one," Daniel said. "Here is a riddle from the fourteenth chapter of Judges. 'Out of the eater came something to eat; out of the strong came something sweet.'"

Jacob shouted, "I know! After Samson killed a lion with his bare hands, a swarm of bees came and made a hive in the lion's body. The answer to the riddle is the honey that came from the dead lion."

The ABC boys cheered and Jacob turned red.

"No big deal," he said, looking at the floor of the tree house.

"Here's a good one," Daniel said. "There are three books of the Bible that if you say their names in order, it makes a sentence."

Every member of the ABC was able to name all sixty-six books of the Bible in order, and this question didn't take long to figure out.

In unison, Mason and Carlos chanted, "Joshua, Judges, Ruth!"

"Yay, ABC boys!" Jacob said.

 **YOUR TURN**

1. There is probably a Bible in your house. Does your family ever read from it?

_____

PRAYER God, how did You squeeze so many cool things into one book? Wow!

STAND BACK, SPIDER-MAN!

Do you love action and adventure? These Bible guys don't have capes, but they seriously rock. Fill in their names and the boxed letters will tell you what these champions have in common. If you haven't heard of these guys, you can find their names by looking them up in your Bible.

1. I fought three hundred men with my spear. (2 Samuel 23:18)

2. I killed a lion in a pit and conquered a giant. (1 Chronicles 11:22-24)

3. I fought six hundred enemy soldiers with only a pointed stick. (Judges 3:31)

4. I used the jawbone of a donkey to defend God's people. (Judges 15:14-16)

5. I destroyed the worship place of the false god Baal and built an altar for the true God. (Judges 6:28-29)

6. The only way my enemies could stop me from preaching for Jesus was to kill me. I was the first Christian to die for Jesus. (Acts 7:58-60)

1. __ __ __ __ [ ] __ __

2. __ [ ] __ __ __ __

3. __ __ __ __ __ __ __

4. __ __ __ __ [ ] __

5. __ __ __ [ ] __ __

6. [ ] __ __ __ __ __ __

A BOOK FULL OF SURPRISES

> **The Bible is full of great stories.**
> *How precious to me are your thoughts, O God!*
> *How vast is the sum of them!*
> **– Psalm 139:17**

BRAIN BURNERS

The members of the Amazing Bible Club sat in a circle in their tree house during sharing time.

Daniel said, "We all know that the first book of the Bible is Genesis and the last is Revelation. But can you list the Bible's books in alphabetical order?"

Several boys grabbed their Bibles.

"Acts is first," Carlos said.

"And Zechariah is last," Mason added.

"So close," Daniel said. "The last book would be Zephaniah."

"Who in the Bible needed the biggest pooper-scooper?" Jacob asked.

"Noah," said Mason. "He had to clean up after all those animals."

"Besides Adam and Eve," Carlos said, "who in the Bible had no parents?"

"Everybody has parents," Mason said.

"I give up," Daniel said.

"Me, too," echoed the other boys.

Carlos grinned wickedly. "The answer," he said, "is Joshua."

"The guy who took over after Moses," Mason said. "He led the people into the promised land. We all know about Joshua, but what makes you think he didn't have any parents?"

Carlos opened his Bible and read. "'In the Book of Joshua, it says that Joshua was the son of Nun.' Get it? The son of *none*."

A wad of paper flew through the air and bounced off Carlos's head.

"What a terrible joke," Daniel said.

"Yeah," Carlos admitted, "but there's nothing terrible about the Bible."

He extended his right hand. The ABC boys circled and piled their hands on top of his. "The Bible is…" Carlos said.

"Amazing!" shouted the rest.

YOUR TURN

1. Do you think you could stump your parents (or your minister) with one of these Bible riddles? Why not give it a try?

PRAYER   God, I know You like having fun. After all, You invented it! Amen.

THE HORRIBLE HAIR DAY

Here's a Bible riddle that is not a joke. In the whole Bible, who had the all-time worst bad hair day? The answer is Absalom, the son of King David. To find out why he had such a bad hair day, you'll have to read the story in 2 Samuel 18:1-18.

Here's a little background to help you with the story. Absalom is the grown son of King David. He is popular, good looking, and known for his long hair. Absalom rebels against his father David to take over the kingdom. The story you're about to read tells the whole tale, check it out to find out what finally happened to Absalom.

WARNING! This story is not for wimps! Rated R for violent content!

After you read the story, draw a picture of Absalom's bad hair day.

■ A SMART HEART ■

When we memorize Bible verses, we store God's word in our heart.

I have hidden your word in my heart that I might not sin against you.
– Psalm 119:11

THE INVISIBLE BIBLE

"I memorize stuff at school," Daniel said. "Why I should memorize verses from the Bible, too?"

"You don't have to," said Jacob, the president of the Amazing Bible Club. "I do it because I like it."

"If I can read the Bible whenever I want," Daniel said, "what's the good of learning parts by heart?"

"I can answer that," Mason said. "Last week in gym class, Mr. Wary was yelling at me for being the last one in the thousand meter run, and he made me run an extra lap. I was mad at him and I was really tired. I wanted to quit running and walk the rest of the lap, but as I ran I remembered one of my favorite memory verses of all time: 'I can do everything through him who gives me strength.'"

"That's Philippians chapter 4, verse 13, right?" asked Carlos.

"Right," Mason said. "I said that verse over and over as I ran. Remembering that God gives me strength kept me from giving up."

"I guess you didn't have a Bible with you on the track," Jacob said.

"Afraid not," Mason said. "There's no pocket in my gym shorts."

"And you'd look kind of silly reading the Bible as you ran around the track," Carlos pointed out.

"So I carry an invisible Bible in the pocket of my heart," Mason said. "Every time I learn a new verse, I store it in my heart. Whether I'm in gym class or taking a test or awake in the middle of the night, that verse is always with me."

"I get it now," Daniel said. "I'm going to start memorizing today!"

1. Can you think of times when you would be glad to know some Bible verses by heart?

God, healthy stuff makes me healthy and unhealthy stuff doesn't. I want to fill my head and my heart with healthy stuff from You. Amen.

THE BEST VERSE EVER?

Some people think that the best verse in the whole Bible is John 3:16. Many people can say it from memory. Do you think you can memorize it? Here are some ways of saying John 3:16 from different translations of the Bible. Pick the one you like best and see if you can learn it by heart.

Tip Number One: Write the verse on a piece of paper, and study it when you have a few minutes on the school bus or while waiting in line at lunch.

Tip Number Two: If you already know John 3:16, pick a new verse to learn. Maybe you can memorize a verse from one of the other stories in this book.

• For God so loved the world that he gave his one and only Son, that whoever believes in him shall not perish but have eternal life. (New International Version)

• For God so loved the world, that he gave his only begotten Son, that whosoever believeth in him should not perish, but have everlasting life. (King James Version)

• For God loved the world so much that he gave his one and only Son, so that everyone who believes in him will not perish but have eternal life. (New Living Translation)

• De tal manera amó Dios al mundo, que ha dado a su Hijo unigénito, para que todo aquel que en él cree no se pierda, sino que tenga vida eternal. (Reina-Valera 1995)

ROOM FOR EVERYBODY

God wants us to care about others.

Do to others as you would have them do to you.
— Luke 6:31

THE TREE HOUSE

"The Amazing Bible Club is the best club I've ever been in," Carlos said.

"I love our tree house," Daniel said. "I feel like we're extra close to God in this maple tree."

Mason cleared his throat nervously. "Can we talk about a new member?"

"Do you know somebody who wants to join?" Jacob asked.

"Sort of," Mason said. "Devon is a guy in my church. He reads the Bible every day. I mentioned our club, and he asked me if he could come to a meeting sometime soon."

"Why didn't you bring him today?" Carlos asked.

"There might be a problem," Mason said slowly. "I don't know if Devon would fit in."

"Why not?" Daniel asked. "He sounds great."

"He is great," Mason agreed. "But he uses a wheelchair."

"So what's the prob—" Carlos began. "Oh, the tree house."

"Maybe we could haul Devon up here," Jacob asked. "Tie a rope around him or something."

"Somebody would get hurt for sure," Carlos said.

"And we don't want him to feel like a suitcase," Mason said.

"Gosh, that's too bad," Daniel said. "I guess there's no way he can join."

"Wait a minute," Carlos said. "Remember the verse we learned about treating others the way we want to be treated?"

"But it's not our fault he can't climb a tree," Daniel said.

"It's not Devon's fault, either," Jacob said.

"Why doesn't he find a club that meets on the ground?" Daniel said.

"Are we just learning the Bible," Carlos asked, "or are we living the Bible?"

"We should vote on this," Jacob said. "Everyone who wants to find a meeting place where Devon can join us, raise your hand."

YOUR TURN

1. What do you think the Amazing Bible Club should do?

_____

PRAYER   God, it's so easy to think about what I want. I'm going to try to think about what other people want, too. Amen.

THE GOLDEN RULE

There were many rules and laws in the days of Jesus. So that we wouldn't have to remember so many rules about how to get along with each other, Jesus gave us one special rule. He said, "Do to others as you would have them do to you." He meant that we should treat other people the way we would like them to treat us. This teaching from Jesus is so important that some people call it the Golden Rule.

Pick five people from your family, your school, and your neighborhood, and put their names on the steps of the ladder. Beside each name write one thing you can do for that person to treat them the way you would like to be treated. Do you think you can practice the Golden Rule with each of these people this week?

KNOCKING AND ASKING

God wants us to ask him for what we need and what we want.

Ask and it will be given to you; seek and you will find;
knock and the door will be opened to you.
– Matthew 7:7

BETTER THAN A TREE HOUSE?

"We're agreed," said Jacob. "We'll invite Devon to join our club."

"Even though it means we can't meet here in the tree house anymore," Daniel said. "But it would be wrong to keep Devon out of the Amazing Bible Club because he uses a wheelchair."

"You guys can come over anytime you want to hang out in the tree house or need a quiet place to pray," Carlos said. "Even if I'm not around, you're welcome in my yard."

"That sounds good," Daniel said. "Still, gathering in someone's living room won't be the same."

"Why don't we turn it over to God?" Mason said. "I know that we don't always get what we pray for, but Jesus said that if we ask, God will give us what we need."

"Good idea," Jacob agree. "Mason, will you lead us in prayer?"

"Lord, we're trying to do the right thing," Mason said, "but it means giving up our clubhouse. If you want us to meet in a living room, that's what we'll do. But maybe you have some cool place picked out for us. Jesus said, 'Seek and you will find.' We're seeking a new clubhouse, Lord, and asking you to find us one. Whatever you work out will be okay with us. Amen."

The rest of the boys said, "Amen!"

"I know God will lead us to someplace way cool," Carlos said.

Mason made a fist and rapped on the floor with his knuckles.

"What are you doing?" Jacob asked.

"I'm doing what Jesus told us to do," Mason said with a smile. "I'm knocking. Now it's God's turn to open the door into our new clubhouse."

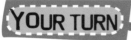
YOUR TURN

1. Do you think God enjoys giving us good things?

_____

_____

PRAYER God, I know I can ask You for anything, and You'll always do what's best for me. Amen.

VOICE MAIL

God has left you a message on your voice mail. Just for fun we've jumbled it up some. You'll need a telephone to figure this one out. On your phone each number has some letters with it. For instance, in this puzzle, the number 2 is either A or B or C. The number 3 is either D or E or F. All you have to do is figure out which letter goes with each number in the message.

2-2-5-5 6-3 2-6-3
4 9-4-5-5 2-6-7-9-3-7

GOD SAYS: ___ ___ ___ ___   ___ ___   ___ ___ ___

___   ___ ___ ___ ___   ___ ___ ___ ___ ___ ___ .

AN OPEN DOOR

God enjoys giving good gifts to his children.
Then you will call upon me and come and pray to me, and I will listen to you.
– Jeremiah 29:12

SETTLING FOR A SHACK

Carlos, Jacob, and Daniel followed Mason to Devon's front door. Mason had been here before, but it was the first time the other members of the Amazing Bible Club would meet Devon.

Mason rang the doorbell and a voice called, "Come in."

They entered the house and found a smiling, blonde boy waiting for them. He rolled forward in his wheelchair and said, "Hi, I'm Devon."

Jacob said, "Devon, we're glad to have you in the club. Mason says you're going to fit right in with this crazy bunch."

"I hope so," Devon said. "I like studying the Bible."

Devon's mother came into the hall and said, "Devon, there is a platter of chocolate chip cookies in the kitchen and a pitcher of lemonade. You can take them to the shack."

"The shack?" Mason asked.

"It used to be a workshop," Devon said. "My dad fixed it up for me. Grab the food and I'll show you."

They went through the kitchen and out the back door.

"Our yard reaches into the woods," Devon said.

Daniel whispered to Jacob, "We traded our super cool tree house for a shack. It's probably filled with spider webs."

"Maybe it won't be too bad," Jacob said, but he looked disappointed.

"I'll bet it has a dirt floor," Daniel moaned softly, "and smells moldy."

They followed a concrete walk that sloped downward.

"It must be hard to roll your wheelchair up this hill," Mason said.

"I've gotten used to it," Devon said. "My arms are strong."

They came around a curve and everyone stopped.

"That's the shack?" Jacob said.

Devon nodded. "What do you think?"

"It's awesome," Daniel said, his eyes wide.

YOUR TURN

1. Should we only ask God for important things?

Even if I just yell, "Help, Lord!" You always hear me. You've got my back! Thanks!

JUST ASK!

God loves giving good things to his children. Ask for what you need and even what you want. Remember that God will decide what's best for you, but you can always ask. Here's what Jesus said about asking for things from God.

Wherever you see a picture, write the word you think goes there. If you need help, you can look up these verses in Matthew 7:7-11.

■ THE MASTER PLAN ■

We cannot imagine the good things God has planned for us.

"For I know the plans I have for you," declares the LORD.
– Jeremiah 29:11

THE NEW CLUBHOUSE

The boys of the Amazing Bible Club stared in amazement at Devon's shack in the woods behind his house.

"Pretty cool, isn't it?" Devon said.

"Cool?" Daniel echoed. "It's below zero."

The shack stood beside a stream, water winding between moss-covered boulders. Ash trees and wildflowers surrounded the shack.

"That's not a shack," Jacob said. "It's a little house."

"Just one room," Devon said. "Lots of space, though. Come on in."

Devon led the way in his wheelchair. He rolled into the shack, and the others followed.

"Wow," Carlos said in a soft voice.

The building had a carpeted floor, and along two walls were shelves that held books and DVDs. Large windows looked into the woods. A flat-screen TV was mounted on one wall. A refrigerator hummed in the corner.

"You've got electricity," Mason said.

"But there's no water in the shack," Devon said. "Sorry, no bathroom."

"Who needs a bathroom when there's a stream?" Carlos joked.

Jacob noticed a door on the back wall. "Closet?" he asked.

"Better than that," Devon said.

The door opened on an outdoor wooden deck with lawn chairs and a small table. Trees shaded it from the sun. The boys could hear the sound of water from a nearby creek. Squirrel and bird feeders hung in the woods.

"We can use this place for our clubhouse?" Jacob asked.

"Sure," Devon said.

"It's a good thing we turned this over to God," Mason said. "This clubhouse is the best!"

"Second best," Daniel said. "God is the best."

1. Is it hard for you to trust God to take care of you? Why or why not?

_____

_____

PRAYER God when You tell me no sometimes, I know it's because You have a better plan for me. When I don't get what I want, help me trust You. Amen.

GOD'S PLAN FOR YOU

God loves you even more than you love yourself. No matter what good things you want, God probably has something better in mind for you. What kind of future do you imagine for yourself? Draw some of your hopes inside the cloud below. It's okay to put in a house or a car, but remember that stuff—even really good stuff—won't make you as happy as friends, family, faith and rewarding work. Do you think you can make this future by yourself or will you ask for God's help?

GOD CAN USE YOU!
God can do great things using anything and anybody.
Then the LORD said to him, "What is that in your hand?"
– Exodus 4:2

STICK TRICKS

"Moses is my favorite Bible story," Devon said.

The Amazing Bible Club was meeting in their new clubhouse behind Devon's house. They sat in lawn chairs on the deck in the afternoon sun.

"He brought the people out of Egypt," Daniel said, "and led them to the Promised Land."

"I like Moses' staff," Devon said. "Think of the things he did with that walking stick."

"Let's see," Carlos said, thinking hard. "He threw it on the ground, it became a snake. That was a sign to prove that Moses was sent by God."

"Right," Devon said. "What else?"

"Didn't Moses use his staff to bring punishments on Egypt?" Daniel said. "Stuff like locusts to eat the crops and fiery hail from the sky."

"Right again," Devon said.

"That's not all," Carlos insisted. "Moses raised his stick in the air and the sea opened up so the people could walk across to the other side."

"I remember another one," Jacob said. "When the people were thirsty in the desert, Moses hit a rock with his stick and water came gushing out."

"That was a fantastic stick," Carlos said.

"Not really," Devon said. "It's God who is fantastic. There was nothing special about the stick. But God did amazing things with it."

The boys nodded and smiled.

"Think about it," Devon said. "If God could overcome Egypt, save Israel, and part the sea with a stick, imagine what God can do with you and me!"

"I don't know," Mason said. "There's nothing special about me."

Daniel said to Mason. "If God can use a stick, then God can even use you."

Everyone laughed, including Mason.

YOUR TURN

1. What talents do you have that God might want to use?

_____

_____

PRAYER Here I am, God. I'm not much, but I'm all Yours. Amen.

WHAT'S IN YOUR HAND?

Moses had a stick in his hand, and God was able to use that stick in amazing ways. What's in your hand? You have things that God can use, too. Maybe it's something you own or something you are good at or something you really like to do. Draw your hand below and on each finger and your thumb write something in your life that God might be able to use. Don't worry about how God can use it, just be honest about the things you can offer to God. If it's a hockey stick, okay. If it's your bug collection or your allowance or your ability to draw, that's okay, too. You won't surprise God, but God might surprise you!

God, here is some stuff in my hand.
You can use it anyway you want to.

Signed: _____

YOUR PERSONAL LIBRARY

Every verse in the Bible is God's gift to us.

All Scripture is God-breathed and is useful for teaching, rebuking, correcting and training in righteousness.
– 2 Timothy 3:16

HEAVY LIFTING

"Behold this fantastic feat of strength," Jacob said to the Amazing Bible Club. "I will lift an entire library with one hand."

The ABC boys cheered and whistled.

Jacob drew a couple of deep breaths, reached out one hand, picked up his Bible, and lifted it over his head.

The ABC boys stomped their feet on the clubhouse floor and shouted their approval. All but Daniel.

As Jacob took a bow, Daniel said, "I don't get it."

"The Bible is one book," Jacob said, "but it's also a library of different books written by many authors."

"Yeah, and there are two rooms in the library," Mason said. "There's the Old Testament with books about Israel and the New Testament with books about Jesus and the church."

"Right," Jacob agreed, "and the Old Testament is a big room. It has stories about Abraham, Moses, David and lots of others. It also has poetry books."

"There are poems in the Bible?" Daniel asked.

"The book of Psalms is made up of poems," said Carlos.

"People in ancient Israel sang the Psalms, so it's kind of a hymn book, too," Devon offered.

"Don't forget the books about prophets in the Old Testament," Carlos said.

"I think I know what's in the New Testament library room," Daniel said. "There are four gospels about the life of Jesus, a book about the beginning of the church, and a lot of letters between early Christians."

"And Revelation, too," Mason reminded. "The book with all the monsters and weird stuff."

"Wow!" Daniel said. "The Bible really is a library in one book."

1. Do you have favorite parts of the Bible? If so, what are they?

_____

God, the Bible is so cool. I could read it my whole life and never get tired of it. Thanks for giving me a book that always feels new. Amen.

LEARNING THE LIBRARY

A library isn't much help if we don't know where to find the books we want. The same is true of the Bible. Did you know that stories about Jesus are found in the Gospels? Did you know that the stories of the first Christians are found in Acts?

Here's a chance for you to learn your way through the library of the Bible. Your Bible probably has a contents page listing all the Bible books in order. Using that list, label these library books and you'll be on your way to learning how to use the Bible. Start with the first book in the Bible—GENESIS—and write that on the first book on the top shelf of the library. EXODUS comes next. Keep going until you reach REVELATION.

This will take some work, but it will be worth it. When you finish filling out this page, you can study how the Bible is put together.

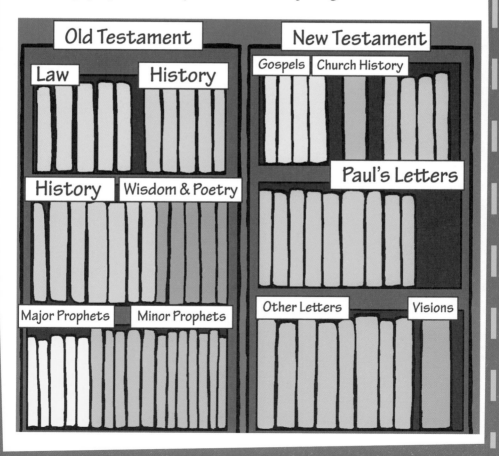

CHAPTER THREE

THE BEST ME
I CAN BE

FACING FEAR

God helps us face our fears.

For God did not give us a spirit of timidity,
but a spirit of power, of love and of self-discipline.
– 2 Timothy 1:7

THE SCARY RIVER

Cass and Elliot tugged on the thick rubber wetsuits. As they emerged from the changing room, Mr. Palmer and the rest of the group awaited them beside the gushing Gauley River as it tumbled and threw spray into the autumn air.

Mr. Palmer said, "Boys, God has given us beautiful weather for our whitewater rafting adventure."

The boys whistled and cheered, except for Cass who stared at the rushing river with wide eyes.

"But first a few rules," Mr. Palmer said.

As the leader explained what to do if someone fell from the raft, Cass felt knots of fear tangling in his stomach. Why had he come on this dangerous trip? He wished he could think of some way to get out of this. Maybe if he pretended to be sick…

Mr. Palmer asked, "Is anybody scared?"

Most of the boys hooted and hollered no.

"You're braver than me," said Mr. Palmer. "On my first rafting trip, I was terrified of falling out of the raft."

Cass tuned in to the man's words. It was hard to believe Mr. Palmer was afraid of anything.

"I fell out of the raft three times in the first hour," Mr. Palmer said, "and it didn't hurt a bit. The things we're afraid of are never as bad as we think."

Cass considered that. He remembered things he had dreaded that turned out to be no big deal. Maybe whitewater rafting would turn out like that, too.

"Pay attention," Mr. Palmer said. "Follow the rules. And remember God is watching over you. Is everybody ready?"

As the other boys yelled, Cass took a deep breath and whispered, "Yeah, God, I'm ready."

YOUR TURN

1. Can you think of a thing you feared that later turned out to be no big deal?

 **PRAYER** God, when I get scared help me remember that You're right here beside me. Amen.

FIGHTING FEAR

Here are some weapons to help you handle fear the next time you're feeling afraid.

TELL GOD ABOUT IT! Talking to God can make us feel much better when we're scared.

USE THE BIBLE! Learn where to find passages in the Bible that will remind you of God's help. Here's a good one: Be strong and courageous. Do not be terrified; do not be discouraged, for the LORD your God will be with you wherever you go. (Joshua 1:9)

LIVE IN THIS DAY! If the thing that scares you is in the future, try not to spend too much time worrying about it. Many of the things we fear never actually happen. Even if it does happen, it probably won't be as bad as it was in your imagination.

REMEMBER YOUR VICTORIES! Remind yourself of the times you have done well in spite of fear. Recall the times God has helped you get through something tough.

GET READY! If there are things you can do to get ready to face your fear, do them. For instance, if you're scared about giving a report in front of the class, practice it first in front of your family.

LOOK FOR HELP! Are there people who can help you? Ask them. Maybe someone knows just what you need to deal with whatever is frightening you.

THE FRONT OR THE BACK?

God doesn't want us to always push our way to the front.
*If anyone wants to be first, he must be the very last,
and the servant of all.*
— **Mark 9:35**

OVERBOARD!

Elliot and Cass climbed into the inflatable raft with four other boys. Mr. Palmer scrambled into the back where he could coach and guide. Elliot sat in front for the best view.

Mr. Palmer surveyed the raft and said, "Elliot, you're new at this. I want you to trade places with Wayne."

"I can do anything Wayne can do," Elliot protested.

Mr. Palmer shrugged. "We'll give you a chance. Just remember, when we get into rough water, you've got to keep paddling."

Elliot said, "You can count on me."

The first few miles on the river were gentle with a few easy patches of bumpy water. Elliot heard a roar ahead and knew they were approaching their first real white water. The air vibrated with the thundering sound.

Mr. Palmer called, "Boys, follow my directions and we'll be fine."

As the water foamed and leaped, Mr. Palmer shouted to paddle right or left.

Suddenly a rock loomed in their path, and the rushing water veered left.

"Everybody paddle hard!" Mr. Palmer shouted. "Don't stop!"

As the water splashed in his face and the front of the boat dipped, Elliot dropped his paddle and grabbed the side of the raft.

"Paddle now!" someone shouted, but Elliot hung on tighter. The raft spun sideways, rose up at one end, and the whole boat flipped upside down spilling everyone into the torrent.

Downstream, they righted the boat and gathered their paddles.

Mr. Palmer asked, "Did we learn anything from that?"

Elliot said, "Yeah, I learned I wasn't ready to be in front."

Mr. Palmer nodded.

"Back in the raft everybody," he said.

 **YOUR TURN**

1. Have you ever tried to do something that was too hard for you? How did it turn out?

_____

PRAYER God, Jesus didn't always try to be first. Help me to be like him. Make me willing to take second place or last place if that's what You want for me. Amen.

BRANCHING OUT

Learning what we can do and what we can't do yet is part of growing up. Like the tree below, you and I are still growing. On the trunk of the tree write some things that you are good at, things you can do without anyone's help. On the roots of the tree, write some things that you can do only with help from others. And on the branches of the tree, jot down some things you can help other people do, like younger kids, for example.

Up the Creek

God wants us to build up one another.
*Carry each other's burdens, and in this way
you will fulfill the law of Christ.*
– Galatians 6:2

Paddle Partners

"I let the whole group down," Elliot said miserably. "When we needed every paddle, I got scared and grabbed the side of the raft. My paddle didn't do much good lying beside me."

The river was straight and smooth here. The boys paddled lazily.

"It could happen to anybody," Mark said. "This is your first time on whitewater, right?"

Elliot nodded.

Mark said, "On my first raft trip, we came into these rapids and water was splashing into the raft. We were bouncing and rolling. Rocks were all around us. The guide was yelling at us to paddle, but I freaked out. I did exactly what you did."

"You grabbed the side of the raft?" Elliot asked.

"Yeah," Mark said, "and I held on like a crab."

Elliot grinned. "Did the raft turn over?"

Mark nodded. "But that wasn't the worst of it. When we went into river, I lost my paddle."

"I guess you found it down stream," Elliot said.

"Nope," Mark said. "It must be on the bottom of the ocean by now. You've heard of being up the creek without a paddle? That was me."

Elliot laughed and slapped his knee.

"I was dead weight," Mark said. "I found a long limb on the bank and tried paddling with that."

Elliot laughed more loudly. "Everybody else had a paddle and you had a stick."

"So cut yourself some slack," Mark told him. "Everybody messes up sometimes. Forget how you did on the last whitewater. What matters is how you do on the next rapids."

"Thanks," Elliot said. "I'm feeling better."

"No problem, partner," Mark said. "We're all in the same boat."

YOUR TURN

1. When you're having trouble, does it make you feel better when someone tries to help?

PRAYER God, when somebody is down, show me how to pick them up. Maybe next time, they'll pick me up. Amen.

I'VE GOT YOUR BACK

Life is a lot easier when we pick each other up and help one another carry the load. Here's a trick you can try with a friend, but the only way this will work is if you carry each other's weight.

1. Sit back to back on the floor with your friend. Lean against each other.

2. Reach back and hook your arms through your friend's arms. Pull your feet close to you. With your arms hooked, each of you must push against the other while rising to your feet. It might take a little practice, but you can get the hang of it. It works best if you and your friend are about the same size. When you get good at this, try it with three!

Remember, sometimes in life we need someone to share the weight with us!

■ ON GOD'S TEAM ■

In God's family, everyone matters.

So in Christ we who are many form one body,
and each member belongs to all the others.

– Romans 12:5

EVERY PADDLE

Mr. Palmer shaded his eyes and stared ahead at the rolling river.

"There's white water around the next bend," he said. "Let's get through this one right side up."

Elliot felt his face grow hot, remembering how he had dropped his paddle and grabbed the side of the raft in the last rough water. Because of Elliot, the whole raft turned over.

"We need every paddle," Mr. Palmer said. "We have to keep the raft moving forward or we can't steer. That means every paddle in the water. Nobody gets to goof off or coast. We're depending on each other. If one of us doesn't do his part, we'll all go swimming."

The sound of the river grew louder as they floated around the bend. Ahead they could see rocks larger than cars poking from the river and foaming water roaring and twisting between the stones. As the water smashed into the rocks, white spray filled the air.

"This is no different from belonging to a team or a family or a church," Mr. Palmer told them. "Everyone has work to do, and we all look out for each other."

He looked around the raft, studying each boy as the water ran faster.

"If you see somebody going over the side, try to grab them and pull them back. I'm counting on Elliot who's counting on Wayne who's counting on Cass who's counting on Mark." He named every boy in the raft. "We're all counting on each other. We do this together or we don't do it."

He paused and smiled.

"Let's all paddle," Mr. Palmer said, "and let's all have some fun."

1. Do you have chores in your house? Do you think it's fair that you have to help with work at home?

_____

God, I can't do everything, but I can do some things. I want to do my part in my family, in my school, and in my church. Amen.

WORKING TOGETHER

Which of these words describes a team effort? Choose the words you think are most important and write them on the paddles that the boys in the raft are using.

COOPERATE - SELFISH - ANGER - REVENGE - LEARNING
SUPPORT - FORGIVE - SHARE - BLAME - LISTENING
APPRECIATION - PRAISE - NAME-CALLING - EFFORT
RESPECT - HELPFUL

HIGH QUALITY

You are wonderful because God made you.

I praise you because I am fearfully and wonderfully made;
your works are wonderful, I know that full well.

– Psalms 139:14

AND IT WAS GOOD!

"It's story time," said Mr. Palmer, poking the campfire. "In the beginning of the world God created everything. On the first day, God created light to shine in the darkness. And it was good. On the second day, God created the sky, and it was good."

The campfire popped and a spark rose into the air, shining against the stars.

"On the third day, God created the land and the plants. And—"

After a moment of silence, Cass said, "And it was good."

"You've got it," Mr. Palmer said. "On the fourth day God made the sun, moon, and stars, and—"

"It was good," the boys chanted.

"On the fifth day, God created swordfish, hummingbirds, whales, and hawks," Mr. Palmer said.

"And it was good!" the boys said in loud voices.

"On the sixth day, God made land animals and people."

"And it was good!" the boys shouted. Their voices echoed across the river.

"That means God made you and me," Mr. Palmer said. "Does God ever do a bad job?"

"No way," Elliot said.

"That's right," Mr. Palmer agreed. "God never messes up. Elliot, you are God's good work. You, too, Wayne. And you, Cass."

He worked his way around the circle, naming each boy in turn.

"When you feel bad about yourself, remember who made you," Mr. Palmer said. "When you feel fat or dumb or clumsy, remember that you are God's good work. When you make mistakes or fail, God doesn't give up on you. Don't give up on yourselves."

"And we're pretty good," Wayne said.

"Yes, you are," Mr. Palmer said.

YOUR TURN

1. Name a few wonderful things about yourself. Share the list with someone you trust.

_____

PRAYER God, You made me, and You don't make junk. Thanks for doing such a good job. Amen.

GOD DOESN'T MAKE JUNK

If God made you, you must be pretty amazing. Nobody else is exactly like you, and nobody else could be you. Congratulations on being who you are! Maybe you don't think very much about how special you are. Try finishing each of these sentences. Don't be shy. Remember, God only makes the best.

A thing that makes me special is:

_____ .

Something my family likes about me is:

_____ .

A game I'm good at is:

_____ .

My friends like me because:

_____ .

A thing I like about myself is:

_____ .

At school, I *do* well in:

_____ .

God is proud of me because:

_____

_____

Made by God

COMPLAINT DEPARTMENT
Complaining only makes things worse.

Finally, brothers, whatever is... excellent or praiseworthy—
think about such things.

– Philippians 4:8

RAW EGGS AND BLACK TOAST

"Wayne is the worst cook in the world," Elliot said.

"The eggs are runny," Cass agreed, "and this toast is so burned, I'm afraid I'll break a tooth."

Wayne shrugged. "I did the best I could," he said. "We'll see if you do better when it's your turn to cook."

"My dog Rocky could cook better than this," Elliot said. "Come to think of it, Rocky eats better than this."

"You look at the bad stuff all the time," Wayne said, "and forget about the good things around you."

"Good things?" Cass asked, scraping away the burned crust from his toast.

"The beautiful view," Wayne said, pointing a fork toward the slopes covered in orange and red trees. "The clean air. The sound of the river."

"And the sound of my stomach gurgling as these raw eggs slide down," Elliot said.

"If you think complaining will make things better, go ahead and gripe," Wayne said. "I'm going to move over there where I don't have to listen."

He took his plate and moved closer to the river.

Cass looked around the camp. He heard the laughter of friends. He saw the sun poking over the hilltops. A fish jumped in the river and came down with a splash. Morning mist floated above the river.

"Wayne's right," Cass said. "This is a great morning, and it's stupid to let a bad breakfast ruin it."

"It's not really that bad," Elliot said, forking eggs into his mouth.

Cass stood up and brushed sand from his pants. "Let's go sit with Wayne."

"Yeah," Elliot agreed, "and no more complaining. Let's focus on the good stuff instead."

"Right," Cass said. "From now on, this river is a no-gripe-zone!"

YOUR TURN

1. Do you know someone who is a complainer? Do you like to spend time with them?

___

PRAYER God, I don't know why I gripe about little stuff when there are so many good things in the world. Give me a thankful heart today. Amen.

SEEING AND SAYING THE BEST

How we say things changes our feelings and the feelings of the people around us. If we complain and moan, everyone will feel bad. If we talk about what's good, everyone will feel better.

Try making these statements better by adding something positive to each negative phrase.

IT'S RAINING, SO I CAN'T GO ON A PICNIC, BUT I CAN _____.

OUR SOCCER TEAM HASN'T WON MANY GAMES, BUT _____.

EVEN THOUGH I DON'T LIKE LANGUAGE ARTS CLASS, _____.

SOMETIMES MY FRIEND BUGS ME, BUT _____.

YESTERDAY WAS AN AWFUL DAY, BUT _____.

BROCCOLI ISN'T MY FAVORITE VEGETABLE, BUT _____.

THE MOVIE I WANTED TO SEE ISN'T AT THE THEATER ANYMORE, BUT _____

_____.

I'M NOT THE FASTEST RUNNER ON OUR TRACK TEAM, BUT _____

_____.

WINGING IT

> ## If we trust God, he will carry us through life.
> *I carried you on eagles' wings and brought you to myself.*
> **– Exodus 19:4**

RIDING ON THE WIND

Elliot and Cass were on clean up duty, washing dishes and pans in a small tub of soapy water.

"This pan is hard to clean," Elliot moaned. "The eggs are burned."

Cass tossed a handful of sand and pebbles into the pan.

"Use the sand like a scrubber," Cass suggested. "Rub it around and it will clean off the sticky stuff."

Elliot rubbed the rough sand into the pan and the burned egg pealed from the skillet.

"Cool!" Elliot said. "That really works."

When they finished, they carried the water a few yards into the woods. There they dug a hole about the size of a football and poured the water in. They kicked dirt back into the hole and covered it with dead leaves.

As they came out of the woods, Elliot pointed into the sky.

"Hey, look," he said, excitement in his voice. "There's an eagle!"

Far overhead, a broad-winged bird moved in a slow circle.

"He's not even flapping his wings," Cass said. "How does he fly like that?"

"He's riding the wind," Elliot said. "When he's that high, he can glide for hours just holding his wings out while the wind does the work."

They stared at the bird in silence for a few minutes.

"Isn't there something in the Bible about God carrying us like an eagle?" Cass asked.

"I don't know," Elliot said, "but it makes sense. If we trust God the way the eagle trusts the wind, then God will carry us along."

"Our trust and God's strength," Cass said. "Kind of like a partnership."

"It's working for the eagle," Elliot said, staring into the sky.

"It works for me, too," Cass said.

YOUR TURN

1. When you carry a puppy or a kitten, would you drop it or let it get

hurt? Do you think God would ever drop you?

PRAYER

God, I'm so glad that no matter how far I go and how high I climb, You're holding on to me and keeping me safe. Thanks! Amen.

FLYING HIGH

God's love carries us just like the wind carries an eagle. Here's a way to make an easy wind rider—a helicopter made from paper. All you need is a three by five inch index card. Or a regular piece of paper will also work. Follow these steps and then drop your helicopter from a high place. As the wind carries it along, remember how God always carries us.

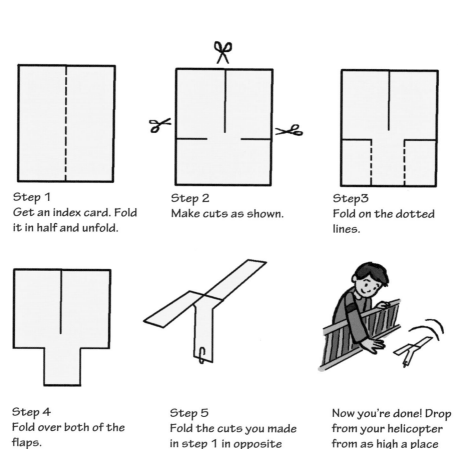

Step 1
Get an index card. Fold it in half and unfold.

Step 2
Make cuts as shown.

Step3
Fold on the dotted lines.

Step 4
Fold over both of the flaps.

Step 5
Fold the cuts you made in step 1 in opposite directions. Attach a paperclip to the bottom.

Now you're done! Drop from your helicopter from as high a place you can and watch it spin as it falls.

■ UNDER COVER ■
God always watches over us.
Because you are my help,
I sing in the shadow of your wings.
– Psalm 63:7

FIERCE FEATHERS

As Cass and Elliot watched the eagle soaring overhead, Mr. Palmer joined them. He scanned the hills, then pointed to one peak.

"See that tree standing by itself?" he said. "That mess of sticks and branches in the top is the eagle's nest."

"Wow," Elliot said. "It's called an aerie, right?"

"Yes," Mr. Palmer agreed.

"It's way up there," Cass said. "I guess nothing could bother the babies that high up."

"There are many hungry animals that can climb that high," Mr. Palmer said. "And other birds that might eat the eggs. That's why the mother keeps a close eye on the nest."

"When there's danger," Elliot said, "the mother eagle spreads her wings over the nest. Nobody's going to get past her."

"That's the way God watches over us," Mr. Palmer said. "Like a mother eagle, God spreads his wings over us."

"God has wings?" Cass asked.

"Not really," Mr. Palmer said. "It's just a way to talk about God's love."

Mr. Palmer glanced at Cass. "It seemed to me you were a little scared when we started this trip," he said. "Is that true?"

Cass nodded. "I was," Cass admitted, "but now I'm having a great time. The next time I'm afraid, I'll remember that God's wings protect me."

"God's wings can even reach under water," Elliot teased. "That's a good thing, because you spend half your time falling out of the boat."

Mr. Palmer and Cass laughed. "Let's get loaded," their leader said. "It's time to get on the river."

"But no matter how many miles we paddle today," Cass said, "we'll still be in the shadow of God's wings."

1. How does it make you feel to imagine that you are a bird in a nest and God's wings are spread over you?

Wow, God! You're always there for me. You've got my back—and my front, and both sides, too! Amen.

SAFE AND SOUND

Decode this message for a promise straight from God's word. Change the numbers into letters. 1 is A, 2 is B, C is 3, all the way to 26 which is Z.

8-5   23-9-12-12   3-15-22-5-18

25-15-21   23-9-20-8   8-9-19

6-5-1-20-8-5-18-19

(Psalm 91:4)

THE RIGHT TEAM
Taking care of the world shows our love for God.
*The earth is the Lord's, and everything in it,
the world, and all who live in it.*
– Psalm 24:1

THE GARBAGE GRABBER

The raft floated slowly down the Gauley River. From a low branch overhanging the water, a squirrel studied them curiously. A red maple leaf drifted in slow circles, landing in the river. The boys were barely paddling, enjoying the autumn afternoon.

Mr. Palmer called, "Paddle right, not too strong."

The boys on the left side of the raft drew their oars out of the water while those on the right paddled. The raft drifted to the left.

"Are we pulling in to shore?" Cass asked.

"No," Mr. Palmer explained. He pointed to a plastic cup floating nearby. "I just want to get that trash. Elliot, would you grab it?"

"It's going to be slimy and nasty," Elliot groaned.

"Maybe a snake is hiding inside," Cass said. He grinned and added, "A slithery, poison snake with big fangs."

"Very funny," Elliot said. "Why can't we leave it floating in the river?"

"Who does this river belong to?" Mr. Palmer asked.

"The state of West Virginia, I guess," Elliot said.

"No, it belongs to God," Mr. Palmer said. "Whoever threw that cup in the water doesn't respect God's ownership."

"A lot of people don't care abut God's creation," Wayne said. "Pollution, littering, using too much fuel… it all makes a mess of the world."

"God's world," Elliot added. He fished the bobbing cup from the water Holding it with two fingers, he emptied it and dropped it into the trash bag.

"Good job," Mr. Palmer said. "There are people who make things worse and people who make things better, Elliot. You just joined the right team."

YOUR TURN

1. What does it mean to you that God owns the world? How would you explain that to someone?

_____

_____

PRAYER God, You made an amazing world for us. I have so much fun outside surrounded by Your world. Help us all to take gift. Amen.

MAKING THE FUTURE

One of the best things we can do for planet Earth is plant more trees. Do you think planting a tree is too hard for you? Think again. Birds and squirrels do it and so can you.

You can plant a tree any time, but fall is especially good because then it's easy to find seeds.

Step One: In your neighborhood or in a park, gather seeds for the kind of tree you want to grow. Maple seeds look like figure A, and oak seeds—acorns—look like figure B. These are both very good trees to grow. Gather about twenty-five seeds.

figure A

Step Two: Choose a place to plant your tree. Don't plant too close to your house or under power lines. A spot that gets sunshine is a good idea. If there is grass there, cut it away with a shovel until you have a circle about one foot wide. Inside the circle, chop the soil with the shovel until it is crumbly.

figure B

Step Three: Plant your seeds a half-inch into the dirt.

Step Four: Wait. Be patient. If you plant in the fall, your seeds will sprout in the spring without any more help from you. If you plant in the spring or summer, you'll need to water it three times a week.

Step Five: When the little trees sprout, select the strongest and biggest. Leave that one in the soil to grow and pull the others out. If you want, you can plant the others in different places or throw them away. Protect your baby tree from shoes and lawnmowers. Keep it well watered.

Step Six: In twenty years, bring your kids and let them climb your tree while you sit in the shade.

NEED SOME HELP?

We can be thankful for people who help us in life.
Share with God's people who are in need.
– Romans 12:13

THE RIGHT WORD

"We did it," Wayne shouted. "All the way through those rapids without turning over or losing anybody."

"Good job," Mr. Palmer said. "I'm proud of you. Everyone followed orders, no one held back. We were there for each other all the way."

"When that big wave hit us from the side," Elliot said, "Cass almost flew over the side," Elliot said. "If I hadn't grabbed his life jacket, he'd have visited the fishies."

Cass said, "You're so full of hot air. I was doing fine, and I didn't need any help from you."

"Yeah?" Elliot said. "How come your eyes were as big as basketballs and your mouth was wide open?"

"Hey, Elliot," Dylan said, "what about when you dropped your paddle and it slid to the back of the raft? If I hadn't kicked it back, you'd have been as useless as a log."

"I could have reached it," Elliot snapped.

"With a ten foot pole," Cass said.

Mr. Palmer cut in, "Sometimes we're better at giving help than accepting help. But everybody needs help sometimes. When you get help you can pretend like you don't need it, or you can fall back on one word."

He paused. "Anybody know what word I mean?"

Cass thought for a moment then turned to Elliot.

"Thanks," Cass said.

Elliot nodded and turned to the other boy.

"Thanks, Dylan," Elliot said.

"That didn't hurt so much, did it?" asked Mr. Palmer.

"Not a bit," Cass and Elliot said at the same time, and both boys laughed.

YOUR TURN

1. Is it easier for you to give help or to ask for help? Why do you think you feel this way?

_____

_____

PRAYER   God, when I need help, it makes me feel weak or dumb. I want to remember that everyone needs help sometimes. Teach me to ask for help when I need it. Amen.

SAYING THANKS

You probably say thank you when someone opens the door for you or passes you the mashed potatoes. But do you ever say thanks for the big things? Have you said thanks to the person who washes your clothes or cooks your meals? Have you said thanks to the person pays the bills at your house? What about your favorite teachers, youth group leaders, and coaches?

Here's your chance to say thank you to some of those people. Use the thank-you-card pattern to the left, or make up your own. Draw on the front and write on the inside. The most important thing is to think of five people you want to thank and to write a short note to each person. When you're finished, you can mail them or deliver them in person!

FOLLOWING RULES

Following the rules keeps us out of trouble.
*Give me understanding, and I will keep your law
and obey it with all my heart.*
– Psalm 119:34

THE GOPHER HOLE

Don't leave the camp without a partner. That was Mr. Palmer's rule. It was an easy rule. So why, Cass wondered, did I have to be such a dummy?

After a full day of white water rafting, Mr. Palmer had steered the boat to a quiet shore where the boys swam, jumped from a tall rock, and made great splashes. After the tents were set up, the leader declared an hour of free time.

"You can rest," Mr. Palmer told them, "or go exploring. Just don't leave camp without a buddy."

So what did Cass do? He went into the woods by himself to see what trees he could identify. He hadn't meant to leave camp. Not really. He planned to go only a few yards into the woods, but before he realized, he had wandered quite far from camp. Just when he decided to turn back, he accidentally stepped into a gopher hole and twisted his ankle. It had swollen like a balloon and soon it hurt too much to walk on it.

Now he sat on the ground with his leg stretched out and his ankle throbbing, waiting for someone to come looking for him. He brushed off the bugs that crawled over his body and watched the shadows grow longer.

"Why didn't I follow the rules?" he said to himself. "If I'd had a buddy I wouldn't be in this mess. I guess there are good reasons for the rules Mr. Palmer gives us."

He heard movement in the dry leaves and voices calling his name.

"I'm here!" he yelled. "Over here!"

Under his breath he added, "The big rule-breaking dummy is over here. Even if Mr. Palmer hollers at me, I can't wait to get back to camp."

YOUR TURN

1. Why do people make up rules? Is it just so they can boss us around?

_____

2. Some rules seem pretty silly, but think of a few rules that make sense.

_____

PRAYER

God, rules can be such a pain, but I know rules are meant to keep me safe and well. Make me smart enough to follow the rules—at least, most of the time. Amen.

WHY RULES?

Most of us don't like rules very much. We forget that most rules are meant to help us live better lives. You'll find out some good reasons for following the rules if you can find the safety words below.

```
T C P W F B L
E N S H A R E
L U A R I Z A
S T F P R U R
O B E Y N E N
```

Share • Obey • Safe • Fair • Learn

■ LIVING AND LEARNING ■

We are always growing in body and spirit.

But grow in the grace and knowledge
of our Lord and Savior Jesus Christ.
– 2 Peter 3:18

TWO DAYS LATER

"Boys, you've done a great job," Mr. Palmer said as the raft bobbed lazily down a calm stretch of river. "We have one more stretch of white water before we reach the landing where our bus is waiting." Mr. Palmer said.

A few of the boys groaned.

"We don't want to go home yet," Wayne said. "This is too much fun."

"Two days ago most of you had never been in a raft, and now you're paddling like experts," Mr. Palmer said with pride. "To show you how much you've learned, I want you to steer the last white water without my help."

Cass and Elliot exchanged worried glances.

"Whoa!" Elliot said. "We can't do that."

"I think you can," the leader said. "Wayne, you take my place here in the back and be the coach. I'll take your paddle and sit in the front."

Wayne carefully moved to the rear, and Mr. Palmer described the upcoming rapids to him and made suggestions about their path.

"Think you can do it?" Mr. Palmer asked.

"I can try," Wayne said.

Mr. Palmer seated himself in the front as the water grew louder.

"Paddle right," Wayne called. "Paddle left. Hard left! Now everybody."

The raft slipped around rocks and a sudden surge spun the boat backwards.

Watching the river over his shoulder, Wayne yelled, "Paddle backwards!" After a stomach-grabbing drop and another spin, the raft emerged from the rapids pointed in the right direction.

Shouts and high fives filled the boat.

"We couldn't have done that two days ago," Cass said.

"No way," Elliot said. "I guess we're bigger now than when we started."

"Wetter, too," Cass said, splashing water on Elliot.

1. How are you different now than a year ago?

_____

God, even when I'm grown up, I hope I never stop growing. You always have new things for me to learn. Amen.

BIGGER AND BETTER

Jesus grew the same way we do. The Bible says that Jesus grew in four ways: in wisdom, in body, in his relations with God, and his relations to other human beings.

In the section below, write some things that show how you are growing in each of those four ways. Here are some examples to get you started. Look through this list, then come up with your own ideas. Remember that some signs of growth might fit in more than one area.

ACTIVITY	BODY	MIND	GOD	OTHERS
Getting taller				
Learning about the Bible				
Moving to a new city				
Doing more chores at home				
ACTIVITY	BODY	MIND	GOD	OTHERS
Getting taller				

CHAPTER FOUR

GET SMART

A CAREFUL TONGUE

It is smart to be careful how we talk.

A man of knowledge uses words with restraint.
– Proverbs 17:27

WORTHY WORDS

Coach said, "Good game, guys. We'll get 'em next time. Remember batting practice on Monday." He asked Shawn, "Give me a hand with the equipment?"

"Sure, Coach," Shawn said.

As they slid the bats into the canvas bag, Coach said, "Shawn, I heard some language in the outfield today that I don't approve of."

Shawn's face turned red.

"I didn't mean to, Coach," Shawn said. "It just slipped out when I dropped that fly ball."

Coach held up his hand to stop Shawn.

"Son, I'm not asking what you said or why you said it," Coach told him. "Some boys use rough language to show that they're cool or tough, but anybody can say those words. There's nothing tough about it."

"Everybody talks that way," Shawn said.

"I don't talk that way," Coach said. "I say what I have to say, and I don't throw in a bunch of bad words. If you use proper language, others will pay more attention to what you say and they'll respect you."

Shawn retrieved a ball near the backstop and dropped it in the bag.

"It's kind of a habit," Shawn admitted.

"Any habit you make," said Coach, "is a habit you can break. I expect the best from my players. Their best effort and their best behavior."

"Yes, sir," Shawn said.

"I'll be listening extra hard for the rest of the season," Coach told Shawn, "to make sure you're doing your best in center field."

Coach slung the equipment bag over his shoulder.

"Some of the guys were going for ice cream," Coach said. "You have time for a double-dip?"

"For sure," Shawn said.

YOUR TURN

1. Do you sometimes say things just to impress others? Do you think it works?

_____

PRAYER

God, the words that come out of my mouth show what's in my heart. Help me stay clean in my thoughts and my words. Amen.

BREAKING FREE

Bad habits are like chains that weigh us down and keep us from being the people we want to be. Unscramble these words to see some ideas for breaking common bad habits.

MONEY MADNESS
Handling money wisely means planning ahead.

In the house of the wise are stores of choice food and oil, but a foolish man devours all he has.
– Proverbs 21:20

BIG SPENDER

"Let's go to the arcade," Cameron said. "We've got time before the movie."

"I'll just watch," Noah said. "I'm a little short on money."

In the Arcade, Cameron drove a race car, shot at tigers in the Wild Safari game, and tried to reach the top of the climbing wall.

"That made me thirsty," he said.

At the food court, Cameron ordered a triple-chocolate malt.

"We'd better get to the theater," Noah said. "We don't want to be late for the best movie of the summer."

"Yeah, Crimson Spider Meets the Earth-Wrecker," Cameron said. "Crimson Spider is the greatest superhero of all time."

In a store window, Cameron spotted a Crimson Spider baseball cap. As they passed a clothing store, Cameron said, "I've gotta have one!"

He pulled Noah into the store and tried on hats of different colors, checking himself in the mirror.

"I like the black one with the red spider-web on the sides," Cameron said. Cameron counted money into the clerk's hand and said, "I don't need a bag. I'll wear it!"

At the theater, they lined up for tickets.

"Movies are expensive," Noah said. "I had to be careful with my allowance so I could afford a ticket."

Cameron pulled two dollars from his pocket.

"Oh, no," he said. "I must have lost some money."

"You've been spending like crazy since we got to the mall," Noah said.

"Can you loan me enough for my ticket?" Cameron asked.

"I don't have enough for two tickets," Noah said.

"What are we going to do?" Cameron moaned.

"I don't know about you," Noah said, "but I'm going to see the movie."

YOUR TURN

1. Have you ever spent your money and then wished you could have it back? Why does that happen?

PRAYER God, sometimes I don't have enough money because I don't use it well. Help me be careful with the money you give me. Amen.

MAKING A MONEY PLAN

Cameron's Aunt Bertha gave him twenty-five dollars for his birthday. Cameron wants to save fifteen dollars to buy the soundtrack CD from *Crimson Spider Meets the Earth-Wrecker* when it comes out next week. Can you help him plan his spending so that he'll have at least fifteen dollars when the CD is released? Circle the things Cameron can spend money on and put an X through the things he shouldn't buy if he wants the CD. Be careful! Make sure he has fifteen dollars left at the end.

A FURRY FRIEND

> ## It is smart to be kind to animals.
> *A righteous man cares for the needs of his animal.*
> **– Proverbs 12:10**

BUTCH'S NEW HOME

"Let's go to the park and practice our soccer moves," Jeff said.

"Why don't we take Butch along?" Gabe said. "He looks lonesome."

Butch was Jeff's dog, a mixed breed with a long face and big, sad eyes. Butch was chained to a tree in Jeff's back yard. At the sound of his name, the dog stirred and wagged his tail hopefully.

"Nah, he'll just get in our way," Jeff said.

"When was the last time you walked him?" Gabe asked. "Does he ever get off that chain?"

"I don't know," Jeff shrugged. "I have better things to do."

Gabe walked over to Butch and rubbed him under the chin. The dog wriggled excitedly and licked Gabe's hand.

"Hey," Gabe called to Jeff, "his water bowl is empty. So is his food bowl. Have you fed him today?"

"Maybe," Jeff said. "I don't remember. He knocked his bowl over and spilled his water. Let him go thirsty for a while. It will teach him a lesson."

"Why did you even get a dog if you weren't going to take care of him?" Gabe asked.

"Chill, man," Jeff said. "It's not a person, okay? It's just a dog."

Gabe shook his head sadly and rubbed Butch's back.

"If you were mine," Gabe said, "I'd take care of you."

"If you want the dumb dog, take him," Jeff said. "My parents won't care. They're tired of him, too."

Gabe's mother had promised he could have a pet soon.

"Do you mean it?" Gabe asked.

"Sure," Jeff said. "He's yours. Now can we go to the park?"

"No thanks," Gabe said. He unchained Butch from the tree and the dog leaped up, licking his face. "I've got better things to do."

YOUR TURN

1. Do you think animals have feelings? Does it matter how we treat them?

▶ **PRAYER**   God, You made all the animals, and You love them. I love them, too, and I'm glad they're around to make the world so good. Amen.

GOOD CARETAKERS

In the story of creation, God made humans the stewards, or care-takers, of all of creation. That includes taking care of animals. For each of the animals pictured below, choose three ways that people can be good care-takers of the animals and write these things on the lines under the pictures. You can choose from the list on this page, ask a friend, or add your own ideas.

Possible ways to care for animals.

• Make sure they have food and water.

• Provide a warm place to sleep

• Provide shade from the sun

• Make sure they get exercise

• Take them to the veterinarian regularly

• Don't throw garbage in the water

• Clean the food bowl

• Play with them

• Brush their coat

• Give them a blanket or pillow

• Protect them from other animals

• Give them toys

■ A CUP OF DISHONESTY ■

Stealing never leads to anything good.

Dishonest money dwindles away, but he who gathers money little by little makes it grow.

– Proverbs 13:11

EIGHTY-NINE CENTS

Shane winked at Ian as they carried their trays to the table in Jumbo Burger Hut.

They set down the trays containing French fries, burgers, and Ian's drink cup. Shane reached into his jacket pocket and casually drew out a Jumbo Burger Hut drink cup.

"I've used this cup like eight times," Shane said quietly.

Ian frowned at him. "What do you mean?"

"I bought a drink here last month," Shane explained, "and kept the cup. I sneak it in and I get free drinks whenever I eat here. Pretty cool, huh?"

"But that's stealing," Ian protested.

"I paid for it," Shane said, "and there's no limit on refills. That's not really stealing."

"Look, you know it's wrong," Ian said, "so don't try to twist this around. If it wasn't wrong, you wouldn't have to hide the cup in your pocket."

"It's hardly costing Jumbo Burger anything. Everybody knows they get their soft drinks cheap and sell them for high prices. So I'm bending the rules a little," Shane said.

"Call it what it is," Ian said. "It's not bending rules; it's stealing."

"You're mad because I thought of it and you didn't," Shane said. "If you're smart, you'll bring your cup back next time."

"I am smart," Ian said. He shook his head. "I'm smart enough to know that you're going to get you in trouble sooner or later. And I'm smart enough to know that I don't want to make myself a thief for eighty-nine cents. My honesty is worth more to me than a medium soft drink."

1. Do you think stealing is okay if it's only a small amount? Why do you think so?

_____

PRAYER   God, keep me honest. Taking stuff that doesn't belong to me costs too much. Amen.

TRICKY BUSINESS

It's tough not to get led off the right path by the little things. Here's a game to help you remember some things that might tempt you to do wrong. Play the game with a friend using a coin. Heads: move forward one space. Tails: move forward two spaces. Use buttons, coins, or rocks to mark your place on the game board.

START

Took Dad's change off the kitchen table. Go Back 1 Space

A guy at school has the latest comic book and you borrowed it without his permission. Go Back 2 Spaces

Cashier gave you too much change & you gave it back. Move Ahead 1 Space

You Walked the Right Path!

Found a ball cap on the playground and kept it. Go Back 2 Spaces

A girl dropped a cool pen and you returned it to her. Move Ahead 2 Spaces

Found sister's lunch money and returned it instead of buying ice cream. Move Ahead 3 Spaces

SEIZING THE DAY

It is smart to work for things we care about.

All hard work brings a profit, but mere talk leads only to poverty.

– Proverbs 14:23

MAYBE TOMORROW

Cole stood on the porch and watched his family drive away to the State Fair. He really thought that Dad would change his mind at the last minute and let Cole go along. No such luck. Cole and his father had made a deal, and Cole didn't live up to his side of the agreement.

A month ago, everybody in the family had been given chores that had to be finished before going to the fair. Cole's younger sister had to clean out her closet. His older sister agreed to sort through the family bookshelf, put the books in order, and get rid of the old ones nobody wanted. Mom would wallpaper the bathroom, and Dad would replace missing shingles. Everybody had a job.

Cole's job was scrubbing the oil stains in the garage and painting the concrete floor. It wasn't such a big job. Getting on his hands and knees to wash off the oil would be a pain, but painting the floor with a long-handled roller might be fun.

But it was summer vacation from school, and Cole liked to take things easy. He slept late every day, spent time with his friends, and did a lot of goofing off. He kept meaning to get the garage floor done, but the weather was hot and he put off the sweaty work. He actually made a start one day, but scrubbing the oil stains made his arm tired and he decided to go swimming instead.

So here he was, left behind, while everyone else went to the fair. He stood before the open garage and considered the job.

Maybe tomorrow, he told himself.

YOUR TURN

1. Some people always get things done, and some put things off. Which kind of person would you like to be?

_____

_____

PRAYER God, I like playing better than working, but I know everybody has to do their part. Help me find time to work now so I can play later. Amen.

MAKING TIME

 o you know how you spend your time? Here's a way to find out. First fill in the blanks below by guessing how much time you think you spend on each activity. After you've written down your guesses, keep track of your time for a few days by jotting down the hours you spend on each thing.

Do you think you'll find some surprises about how you use your time? Maybe you'll get ideas of better ways to use your time.

JOURNAL OF HOW I THINK I USE MY TIME

TIME SPENT AT SCHOOL _____ hours

TIME SPENT DOING CHORES _____ hours

TIME SPENT WATCHING TELEVISION _____ hours

TIME SPENT WITH MY FAMILY _____ hours

TIME SPENT DOING HOMEWORK _____ hours

TIME SPENT SLEEPING _____ hours

TIME SPENT WITH FRIENDS _____ hours

JOURNAL OF HOW I REALLY SPEND MY TIME

TIME SPENT AT SCHOOL _____ hours

TIME SPENT DOING CHORES _____ hours

TIME SPENT WATCHING TELEVISION _____ hours

TIME SPENT WITH MY FAMILY _____ hours

TIME SPENT DOING HOMEWORK _____ hours

TIME SPENT SLEEPING _____ hours

TIME SPENT WITH FRIENDS _____ hours

GOOD NEIGHBORS

It is smart to treat others with kindness.

He who despises his neighbor sins,
but blessed is he who is kind to the needy.

– Proverbs 14:21

CHOCOLATE COVERED LOVE

As soon as the door opened, Philip said, "Hi, I'm selling chocolate bars to raise money for new uniforms for our marching band."

"Aren't you the boy who scraped the snow off my sidewalk last winter?" Mrs. Colan asked. "I'll buy five chocolate bars."

At the next house, a boy opened the door and said, "Wait a sec."

Philip could hear the boy's voice inside the house. "Phil's selling stuff for the band. Yeah, the guy who helped me with math."

The boy returned to the door. "Mom says we'll buy two."

At the next house, a bearded man opened the door.

"Hi, Dr. Romita," Philip said. "Has your dog turned up?"

"Not yet," the man said sadly. "But thanks for helping me look for him."

Dr. Romita pulled a wallet from his back pocket and took out a ten dollar bill. "I'm allergic to chocolate, but let me make a donation."

When Philip got home, his mom asked, "How did it go?"

"Great," Philip said. "I sold three cases of chocolate bars. People in our neighborhood are so nice."

His mom laughed.

"Philip," she said, "our neighbors are nice to you because you are so nice to them. You are always raking leaves, walking dogs, running errands."

"I just like being a good neighbor," Philip said.

"When you are nice to your neighbors, they'll be nice to you," his mom said. "Love is like a boomerang. It usually comes back."

"Not always," Philip said. "Old Mrs. Buscema said she'd turn her dog loose on me if I bothered her again."

His mom shook her head, but Philip smiled and said, "We still have a bunch of nice neighbors who really like chocolate."

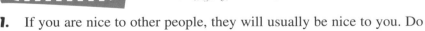

YOUR TURN

1. If you are nice to other people, they will usually be nice to you. Do you think that's really true?

_____

PRAYER   God, life is like a boomerang. Sometimes the kindness I do comes back to me. What a great way to live! Amen.

Super Kindness

Make up names for these superheroes of kindness. Be creative! For instance, the first one might be Helpatronic or Handy-Boy. After you've named each hero, put an number on the scale from 1 to 10 to show much you are like (or not like) that hero.

_____ is always willing to help when someone needs a hand opening a door, carrying a big stack of books, or figuring out the instructions on a math work sheet.

This describes me:

1_____10

    Not at all   Sometimes   Always

_____ does things that need doing before he is asked to do them. People at his house are always wondering: Who folded the clothes for me? Who packed a lunch for me? Who fed the dog? Who found my missing glove?

This describes me:

1_____10

    Not at all   Sometimes   Always

_____ wants everyone to know whenever he does something nice. He makes sure other people see it or hear about it whenever he is kind to someone. He always wants credit for his efforts and good deeds.

This describes me:

1_____10

    Not at all   Sometimes   Always

FIGHTING WORDS

Others will pay more attention to us when we speak with kindness.
The wise in heart are called discerning,
and pleasant words promote instruction.
– Proverbs 16:21

HAIRY SOAP

"I told my sister to stop acting like the Queen of the World," Luke said to his friend Al. "If she keeps on leaving dirty clothes and wet towels in the floor in our bathroom, I told her I'll throw her clothes out the window."

The friends were walking home from a neighborhood football game on a bright fall afternoon.

"She blew up big time. Total supernova," Luke said. "And of course it turned into a major fight."

Al thought about it as they walked along.

"Maybe you could have been nicer when you talked to your sister about her underwear piling up in the bathroom," Al suggested.

"Now you're on her side?" Luke asked.

"Nope," Al said. "But did the fight make things any better?"

"Nah," Luke admitted. "How do you think I should have done it?"

"I don't know," Al said. "Maybe start out with a compliment?"

"Like the way she scrubs the shower every Saturday because she's scared goofy of mold and stuff?" Luke asked.

"Yeah, but leave out the goofy part," Al said. "Start with something you appreciate before you bring up the towels on the floor."

"I guess that makes sense," Luke said. "What else?"

"Instead of saying you'll throw her clothes in the back yard," Al said slowly, "you could offer to do something for her."

"She hates it when I leave hair stuck on the soap," Luke admitted, scratching his head. "Do you think if I'd been nicer, she wouldn't have had a meltdown?" he asked.

Al shrugged and spread his hands. "Sometimes how we say things matters more than what we say," he said.

"Especially with sisters," Luke agreed.

YOUR TURN

1. What can you do to make it easier for others to listen to what you have to say?

_____

PRAYER   Lord, remind me to talk to other people the way I want them to talk to me. Amen.

NOT JUST FOR GROWN-UPS

Maybe you think it doesn't matter how you talk to people while you are young, but the Bible says that it does matter. Decode the words below and put them in the blanks to read the verse from I Timothy 4:12.

Change the w's to e's; Change the x's to o's; Change the m's to l's; Change the b's to t's; and Change the d's to i's.

Yxung	Spwwch	Mdfw
_____	_____	_____
Mxvw	Fadbh	Purdby
_____	_____	_____

Don't let anyone look down on you because you are _____, but set an example for the believers in _____, in _____, in _____, in _____, and in _____. I Timothy 4:12

■ FAMILY MATTERS ■

It is smart to know that some things matter more than money.

*Better a dry crust with peace and quiet than
a house full of feasting, with strife.*
– Proverbs 17:1

THE BIG DINNER

"Ryan has invited me to dinner at his house tonight," Jared told his mom.

"I'll phone his mother to make sure it's okay," Mom said.

"Ryan's family lives in a huge house in Country Squire Estates," Jared said. "They even have a maid and a cook."

"So do you," his mother said with a wink. "Her name is Mom."

"What are you cooking tonight?" Jared asked.

"Meat loaf," Mom said.

"Hah! We'll have something better at Ryan's house," Jared said.

"Let me know if you decide to move in," Mom said. "I'll bring your clothes over."

The dinner was as good as Jared had hoped. Ryan's family had steak and mashed potatoes with cheese and bacon bits. They used fancy glasses on a table too big to fit into Jared's house. Dessert was a triple layer chocolate cake with pudding in the middle.

Better food than at home, Jared decided, *but not as much fun*. He thought about the laughing and joking that went on during dinner at his home. Dad was always kidding Mom about her cooking. Jared and his brothers told funny stories from school. When Mom wasn't looking, Dad would sometimes flick peas across the table. It wasn't unusual for Jared to laugh so hard that milk squeezed from his nose.

Ryan's parents were very quiet. Hardly anyone said a word during the meal. No joking. No messing around. No laughing. By the time dessert was served, Jared felt sorry for Ryan and wanted to leave.

"How was dinner?" his mother asked when she picked him up at Ryan's.

"Okay, I guess," Jared said. "Hey, is there any leftover meatloaf?"

1. Will a big house make a happy family? Why do you think that?

_____

God, I don't have everything, but I have a lot. Teach me to be thankful for what I have and to enjoy everything you give me. Amen.

MY HOUSE

Pretend that this is a picture of your house or apartment. Inside, draw the members of your family and other people that you care about. If there's any extra room, draw some of your favorite things.

God, thank you for...

BRAGGING AND BOASTING

Smart people don't have to talk about how smart they are.

Let another praise you, and not your own mouth;
someone else, and not your own lips.

– Proverbs 27:2

THE CAPTAIN

"I'm very proud to accept this trophy," Hunter said. "As captain, I worked hard to take our academic team to the championship."

The six members of the academic team stood on the stage during a school assembly. The principal was presenting them with their award for winning first place in rapid recall.

"He built our team?" Sophia whispered to Sam. "He missed half of our practice debates and he goofed off when he did show up."

"This season, you answered twice as many questions as he did," Sam said.

The principal glanced in their direction.

"I decided that running drills in different subjects would get us ready for the season," Hunter said. "It was my strategy that helped us make it to the championship."

Sophia turned red. "Hey, that was my idea," she said under her breath.

The principal leaned toward Hunter and said, "Remember the championship was a team victory."

"Absolutely," Hunter said, beaming. "I was too sick to attend one match. The team somehow managed a win even without my leadership."

"I'm going to barf if he keeps this up," Sophia whispered.

The principal said, "Hunter, maybe you'd like to demonstrate how you led the team to victory. Tell us the speed of light."

"Sure," Hunter said. He turned to the team. "Who knows the answer?"

All five team members raised their hands.

"Captain," the principal said, "Answer the question."

Hunter looked uncomfortable. "I think someone else should answer."

"Hunter, I guess you don't want to show off," the principal said.

"Yeah, that's it," Hunter agreed. "I can't stand show-offs."

YOUR TURN

1. How do you feel about people who praise themselves?

_____

_____

PRAYER God, help me to do my best without talking about it. Amen.

BUILD UP OR TEAR DOWN?

Often people tear other people down in order to build themselves up. Change these destructive sentences to constructive statements.

This team would be nothing without me.

_____
_____
_____

Too bad you didn't have this great idea.

_____
_____
_____

Everyone knows I'm the best math student.

_____
_____
_____

Mom always has to depend on me for help around the house.

_____
_____
_____
_____

BORROWING TROUBLE

Borrowing more money than we can pay back isn't smart.

The rich rule over the poor, and the borrower is servant to the lender.

– Proverbs 22:7

THE NOTEBOOK

"Let's go swimming," Tyler said.

"I thought you were broke," Nat said.

"I'll borrow the money from my brother Zach," Tyler said.

Nat followed his friend to his big brother's room. Zach lay on his bed reading a history book.

"What's up?" Zach asked.

"I need a loan," Tyler said, "to get me into the swimming pool. I'll pay you back in a couple of days."

"You always say that, but you never do it," Zach said. He rolled off the bed and picked up a small notebook. Opening it to the first page, he passed it to Tyler. "I've been keeping track of your loans."

Tyler's eyes grew large as he studied the list of loans, amounts, and dates. "I owe you fifty-three dollars? That can't be."

"That's what happens when you keep borrowing and never pay anything back," Zach told him. "Here's what I'll do. I'll let you earn the money for swimming. I'm supposed to cut the grass today. You do it for me and wash my car, then I'll pay your way into the pool."

"All that work for two dollars?" Tyler sputtered. "That's a rip off. I won't do it."

"I guess I'll have to show Dad my loan book," Zach said.

"I'll be grounded until I pay back every penny," Tyler groaned. "That could take all summer."

"Be sure to sweep the drive after cutting the grass," Zach said, "and don't forget to give my tires a good scrub." He lay back on the bed and retrieved the history book. "If you work fast, you can still make it to the pool for a couple of hours."

YOUR TURN

1. What do you think Tyler should do?

_____

_____

PRAYER

God, spending money is okay, but spending money I don't have will get me into trouble. Teach me to be smart about working, spending, and saving. Amen.

MANAGING MONEY

Money is one of the resources God gives us to help us get the things we need. If we're lucky, we have some left over for things we want. How do you manage your money? Do you give 1/10 (that's called a tithe) to the church for God's work? Add up the money below and then figure out where your money is going.

Total Savings $ _____

For every ten dollars I get:

I give _____ to church.

I spend _____ on things for school.

I spend _____ on games and movies and entertainment.

I save _____ for _____.

I spend _____ for _____.

TELL IT LIKE IT IS

Being smart means telling the truth.
The LORD detests lying lips,
but he delights in men who are truthful.
– Proverbs 12:22

THE RED TRUCK

The Scout Master, Mr. Starlin, turned to Dan and asked, "Could your father bring his truck to help us with the grocery drive?"

"His truck?" Dan asked.

"The red truck with the racing stripes," Jake said, nudging Dan and laughing. "Double cab, extra long bed. It's all you've been talking about for a month."

"Sure," Dan said nervously. "Yeah, I'll ask Dad if he can help."

After the meeting, waiting in the church parking lot for their parents, Jake said, "Maybe your Dad will pick you up in the truck tonight. I'd love to look it over."

"I don't think he will," Dan said. "Uh, Dad sold the truck."

Jake turned and looked at his friend in the glow of the parking lot lights.

"Oh my gosh, Dan," he said, "you made the whole thing up. Your dad never bought a truck, did he?"

"He was thinking about buying one," Dan said weakly.

Jake threw his hands in the air. "Why do you lie all the time?" he asked.

"I thought it would be cool if my Dad had a big, red truck," Dan said. "Then I kind of told some people that he did."

"Now you're in trouble," Jake said. "What are you going to tell Mr. Starlin?" Jake asked.

Dan said, "I'll tell him Dad is going to be out of town."

"And what if Mr. Starlin bumps into your dad at the bowling alley and brings up the truck?" Jake asked.

"I'll tell Dad that Mr. Starlin has me mixed up with another kid whose father owns a truck," Dan said.

Jake shook his head.

"Lies to cover up lies," Jake said. "Isn't it easier to just tell the truth?"

YOUR TURN

1. Have you ever told a lie? Did it make things better or worse?

PRAYER   God, sometimes lying would be easy, but I know the truth is always better. Keep me truthful so I can be the kind of person you want me to be. Amen.

WHY LiE?

People have all kinds of excuses for lying. Take a look at the lies below and match each one with a reason why someone might tell that lie.

There aren't right or wrong answers on this one. Just match them the way it makes sense to you.

LIES

I DIDN'T THROW THE BALL THAT BROKE THE WINDOW.

MY DAD COULD GET TICKETS TO THE GAME IF HE WANTED TO.

I DIDN'T GET A GOOD GRADE ON THE TEST.

THE DOG ATE MY HOMEWORK.

I LOST MY LUNCH MONEY.

I WANT PEOPLE TO LIKE ME.

OTHER PEOPLE ASK ME TO LIE.

I DON'T WANT TO LOOK DUMB.

I'M AFRAID OF BEING PUNISHED.

PEOPLE MIGHT MAKE FUN OF ME.

EXCUSES

Do you think any of these are good reasons for lying? What advice would you give to a friend who tells lies so that people will like him?

_____

_____

■ SPREADING RUMORS ■

It is not smart to pass around rumors.

The words of a gossip are like choice morsels;
they go down to a man's inmost parts.
– Proverbs 18:8

GET WELL SOON

On the bus ride home after school, Rob told Kevin, "I don't think I'll make it to choir practice tonight. I've got a stomach ache. Maybe I ate too much lunch."

Walking home from the bus stop, Kevin bumped into BJ, and said, "Rob is pretty sick. I think he has food poisoning."

When BJ got home, he told his sister, "You know that kid Rob? He got food poisoning in the school cafeteria. I'm sure glad I took my lunch today."

Rob's sister called her friend Kim and said, "Did you hear that BJ's friend Rob is in the hospital with food poisoning? They're probably pumping his stomach."

Kim told her mother, "Remember that boy Rob who sings in the church choir?" Kim lowered her voice, "He's in Intensive Care at the hospital. I heard he's having surgery."

Kim's mom went to her car and drove straight to Rob's house. When Rob's mother opened the door, Kim's mom said, "Joyce, I heard about Rob. Is there anything I can do?"

Just then Rob joined his mother at the door. "Hi, Mrs. Allard," he said. Then he said to his mom, "I'm going to choir practice."

"I thought you had a stomach ache," his mother said.

"It's gone," Rob said. "I feel fine now."

He slipped between the women and trotted down the walk, humming under his breath.

Rob's mother turned to Mrs. Allard.

"What did you hear about Rob?" she asked.

Mrs. Allard looked embarrassed.

"Never mind," she said. "You don't want to know."

YOUR TURN

1. Have you ever heard a story that turned out to be untrue? How do you think those stories get started?

_____

PRAYER

God, gossip and rumors cause trouble. I don't want to be a gossiper. I want to tell the truth. Amen.

CRAZY TALK

Ask some friends or family members to help you finish these sentences. Without reading the sentence aloud, ask someone to give you a word to fill in the blank. When you finish, read the sentences back to your friends. If you want, you can make up some more crazy sentences.

Notice that changing just one or two words can make a big difference in what you say about another person.

_____ is a _____ friend.
(name of person)   (descriptive word)

He acts like a/an _____ whenever
(name of animal)

we go out to eat. His favorite food is
_____. In the lunch
(name of vegetable)

room, he always eats pudding with his
_____. Sometimes he carries
(name of body part)

_____ in his pocket as a
(a squishy food)

snack. Maybe he belongs in a
_____!
(place where people go
with their familiities)

WINNING THE FIGHT

It is dumb to let anger control us.

A fool gives full vent to his anger,
but a wise man keeps himself under control.

– Proverbs 29:11

THE HOT HEAD

"You're the worst captain in the whole world!" Rico shouted.

"I make some mistakes," Juan admitted, "but I'm doing my best."

"You shouldn't have benched me," Rico said. "With my fielding, we could have won this game."

"Rico, you were limping after you slid into third," Juan explained. "I decided you should stay off that foot for a while."

Rico held up his fists. "I'll show you how hurt I am. Come on! Try me!"

The other players gathered around Rico and Juan. They started chanting, "Fight! Fight! Fight!"

"Knock it off," Juan said in a loud voice. "There's not going to be a fight. Rico, go home and cool off. We'll talk about this later."

"You're afraid to fight me," Rico said.

"Think what you want to," Juan said. "Go home now."

Rico walked away, making chicken noises in his throat. The other boys laughed and drifted away, leaving only Juan and his best friend Chuck.

"Man, you should have knocked him on his can," Chuck said.

Rico took a deep breath and let it out slowly.

"I already won the fight that mattered," he said.

"What do you mean?" Chuck asked.

"The fight inside of me," Juan said. "Rico really made me mad. I wanted to punch his lights out. But then he and I would end up in the principal's office, and we'd both be kicked off the team. Nobody wins then. I decided I wouldn't let anger tell me what to do."

"Wow," Chuck said. "It's tough when you have to fight yourself."

"You said it," Juan agreed. "But I won."

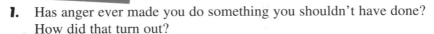

YOUR TURN

1. Has anger ever made you do something you shouldn't have done? How did that turn out?

_____

PRAYER

God, I don't want anger telling me what to do. Help me use my head and keep me out of trouble. I'm going to be in charge of my own life. Amen.

KEEPING ANGER UNDER CONTROL

It's not easy to keep anger from controlling our actions. Find the best path through the maze and discover how you can remain in control even when things go wrong.

CHAPTER FIVE

UNBREAKABLE PROMISES

GOOD COMPANY
Others may leave us, but God never does.

So do not fear, for I am with you; do not be dismayed,
for I am your God. I will strengthen you and help you.
— Isaiah 41:10

THE LONELY HOUSE

"How's my favorite grandson?" Grandpa said, opening the door for Tanner.

"You say that to all your grandkids," Tanner said.

"One favorite just isn't enough," Grandpa said with a wink.

A few minutes later, Tanner and his grandfather were seated at the kitchen table with bowls of cookie dough ice cream.

"This is my favorite ice cream," Grandpa said.

Tanner let a spoonful melt in his mouth. "It seems kind of funny here without Grandma," he said.

"I sure do miss her," Grandpa agreed. "I can hardly believe it's been six months since she died."

"Does it get lonely here without her?" Tanner asked.

"I miss her every day," Grandpa said. "After all, we were married sixty-three years. But I don't get lonely very often."

"How come?" Tanner asked.

"I've known the Lord even longer than I knew your Grandma," Grandpa said. "He keeps me company."

Tanner took another bite of ice cream. He couldn't think of anything to say.

"God is always with his children, even outside of church," said Grandpa.

"Can you feel him?" Tanner asked.

"Sometimes I feel he's close by, but not always," Grandpa said.

"So how can you be sure he never leaves you?" Tanner asked around a mouthful of cookie dough ice cream.

"He promised never to leave us," Grandpa said. "When the Lord says, 'I am with you,' I know he means it."

"So even when you can't feel God close, you still believe it?" Tanner asked.

"Yep," said Grandpa. "Now finish that bowl of ice cream. I've got a couple more favorites I want you to try."

YOUR TURN

1. Do you think God is always with us? Why?

_____

PRAYER | Thanks for being around, God, even when I'm too busy to notice. Amen.

NEVER ALONE

Even if we get lonely sometimes, Jesus is still with us. Although we can't see it, we know the air is there. Jesus is always there, too.

This picture shows some activities you might do sometimes. Connect the dots to help you remember that you are never alone.

NOT THE END

God has promised his children a place in heaven.

Jesus said to her, "I am the resurrection and the life.
He who believes in me will live, even though he dies."
– John 11:25

HEAVEN AND ICE CREAM

Tanner dug his spoon into a mound of marshmallow peanut-crunch ice cream. He always got ice cream at Grandpa's house, but that's not why he visited. Since his grandmother died, Tanner worried about Grandpa being all alone in the house.

"Knowing that God is right here with me keeps me from getting too lonesome," Grandpa said, "even though I do miss your grandma."

"Grandma used to say that, too," Tanner said.

"Oh, yes," Grandpa said. He sprinkled chocolate bits over his own bowl of ice cream. "Your grandma believed in God's promises."

"I wish God had saved her from that stroke," Tanner said.

"Me, too," Grandpa agreed. "But I have a promise that turns sadness into happiness."

"What promise is that?" Tanner asked.

"Heaven," Grandpa said with a wide smile. "Death wasn't the end of Grandma, and it won't be the end of me."

"What is heaven like?" Tanner asked.

"No more getting old," Grandpa said. "No more sickness. No more being sad and lonely. No more tears. God knows what we need to be happy, and God will give us everything we could ever dream of."

"If God built heaven," Tanner agreed, "it has to be super great. But how do you know it's real?"

"I have to keep telling you that God never breaks a promise," Grandpa said. "When Jesus says that He's going to heaven to make it ready for us, He's not just pretending. He means what He says. God never goes back on His word."

Tanner spooned the last of his ice cream, chasing sprinkles around the bowl.

"Will there be ice cream in heaven?" Tanner asked.

"Heaven without ice cream?" Grandpa chuckled. "No way."

YOUR TURN

1. What do you think heaven will be like?

_____

PRAYER

God, sometimes I get scared when I think about death. It helps to know that You have a place waiting for me. Amen.

THE BEST PLACE

We won't know exactly what heaven is like until we get there someday. When you imagine heaven, what comes into your head? What do you think would make you happy forever?

Try putting your imagination into words. Write a word, phrase, or idea about heaven that starts with each letter below.

H _____

E _____

A _____

V _____

E _____

N _____

UNFINISHED

God isn't finished with us yet.

Being confident of this, that he who began a good work in you will carry it on to completion until the day of Christ Jesus.
– Philippians 1:6

SHOOTING HOOPS

Jeff was practicing free throws in the church gym when Pastor Phil came in. "You shoot and I'll rebound," the minister offered.

Jeff's next free throw dropped cleanly through the hoop.

"Nothing but net," Pastor Phil said.

"I wish everything came as easy as basketball," Jeff said.

"Yeah?" Pastor Phil said. "Sounds like you're struggling with something."

"I haven't been a Christian very long," Jeff said.

"I remember," said Pastor Phil. "I baptized you last year."

"Following Jesus is harder than I thought it would be," Jeff said.

Jeff dribbled twice, then raced in for a lay up. The ball banked into the basket and Jeff caught it.

"What's hard about it?" Pastor Phil asked.

"I thought I'd change faster," Jeff said. "Some of my bad habits don't want to let go."

Pastor Phil nodded. "Sometimes my temper flares up or I say something mean, and I think, 'Where did that come from?'"

"You, too?" Jeff asked. "I thought you were perfect."

Pastor Phil laughed. "My friends will tell you how imperfect I am," he admitted. "Do you know what keeps me from giving up?"

Jeff shook his head.

"I remember that God isn't through with me yet," Pastor Phil said. "Even when I fail, God doesn't. I have God's promise that he will help me become everything I should be."

"So God is still making me into his child?" Jeff asked.

"Yes, and God never quits until the job is done," Pastor Phil said,

The minister took a shot from the free throw line. The ball rolled around the rim twice before dropping in the net.

"Not too bad," Jeff said. "For a pastor."

 **YOUR TURN**

1. Are there things you'd like to change about yourself? Do you think God will help you?

▶ **PRAYER**   God, I'm not who I want to be yet, but I know You'll finish what You've started in me. Amen.

CAUTION: GOD AT WORK

God is still working on you and me and our world. You are a masterpiece, but you aren't finished yet. God will make sure you grow into everything you should be, and you can help by following God's rules, praying, and reading the Bible.

This picture of a basketball game isn't finished yet, either, but you can help that, too. Look for the missing parts of the picture and draw them in.

■ BAD NEWS, GOOD NEWS ■

Someday, God will bring peace to the world.

They will beat their swords into plowshares and their spears into pruning hooks. Nation will not take up sword against nation, nor will they train for war anymore.

– Isaiah 2:4

TELEVISION TENSION

Ted sat in the family room reading his Bible, while his father watched the evening news. Ted glanced up from the pages of his Bible and saw a news clip of rockets falling on a city in the Near East. A newscaster explained that one missile had destroyed a school and killed four children.

Ted tried to return to his reading, but the television distracted him.

The news shifted to a country in a different part of the world where citizens were in the streets protesting against the wrongdoing of their government. The government sent soldiers to break up the crowds, and violence flared up. The protesters threw rocks and bottles while soldiers fired rifles into the crowd. Protesters lay on the pavement. Some moaned in pain, while others were utterly still.

"The death toll," announced the newscaster, "is estimated at thirty seven."

During the station break, Ted began reading again. But again the news caught his attention when a reporter described an African nation where one tribe wanted to destroy another.

Suddenly the TV went blank and silent. His father, holding the remote, said to Ted, "Nothing but bad news on television." He waved at the Bible in Ted's lap. "Any good news in there?"

"It says here that someday God will bring peace to the whole world," Ted said. "No more killing or hurting. Even the animals will be at peace. Little kids will play with snakes. Lions and lambs will nap together. Cows and bears will be buddies."

Ted read, "They will neither harm nor destroy on all my holy mountain." His father closed his eyes and smiled.

"Read some more to me," he said. "I can use some good news."

1. Why do you think there is so much violence in the world?

_____

God, I know that even though I can't see You, You're still there all the time. Thank You for always being there. Amen.

THE KINGDOM OF PEACE

When God's Kingdom comes, there will be no more fighting or killing, only peace among all people and creatures.

If the Kingdom of God had a flag, what do you think it would look like? Would it show a picture of peace? Would it have a cross? Would it have words on it? Draw what you think in the flag below.

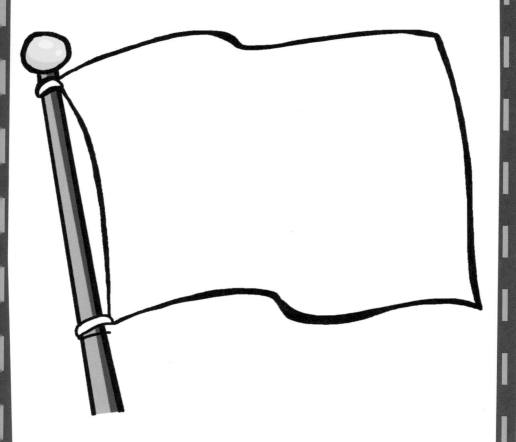

NO MATTER WHAT

God is bigger and stronger than our problems.

And my God will meet all your needs according to his glorious riches in Christ Jesus.

– Philippians 4:19

ROCKS IN THE STREAM

"We might have to move," Neil said. "My dad is probably going to lose his job soon."

"That stinks," Josh said.

Neil turned over a large rock in the stream, looking for snakes or crawfish.

"Are you scared?" Josh said.

"A little scared, I guess," Neil admitted. "Mom says I shouldn't worry."

"Because your dad can find another job?" Josh said.

"No, because God will take care of us," Neil said.

"Cool," Josh said. "So you won't have to move."

"I don't think it works that way," Neil said. He lifted another rock and a snake darted into the current.

After the snake disappeared, Josh said, "My family doesn't go to church, so I don't know much about God. Will he take care of you or not?"

Neil thought about it for a while.

"Yes, God will take care of us, but we still might have to move," he decided.

"I don't get it," Josh said.

"God doesn't always keep our family from having trouble," Neil said, "but God always gets us through the trouble.

Josh hoisted up a large rock in both hands and threw it into the middle of the stream. A huge splash threw water into the air.

"Maybe it's like this stream," Neil said. "All these big rocks and dead trees get in the way of the stream. The water has to change course, move around things, push past stuff, but it still gets where it's going. It'll be like that with my family. Things might get bumpy, but God will make sure we keep going."

"I hope you don't move," Josh said.

"Me, too," Neil said. "But whatever happens, I know God will watch over us."

YOUR TURN

1. Do you ever worry about problems that might come? Does worrying make things better or worse?

 God, I know things are not always going to turn out the way I want, but I trust You to get me through. Amen.

ENGiRCLED BY LOVE

God gets us through our hard times, no matter how big our troubles seem to be. God's love wraps around us like a hug and keeps us safe. This word circle has an important message for every Christian. Start with the green G at the top of the circle and moving to the right, read every other letter. When you have gone twice around the circle, you will have the whole message.

__ __ __ __ __ __ __ __ __ __ __

__ __ __ __ __ __ __ __ __ __ __

__ __ __ __ __ __ __ __ __ ___!

READY FOR THE STORM

We always have a safe place in the hands of God.

The LORD is my rock, my fortress and my deliverer;
my God is my rock, in whom I take refuge.
He is my shield and the horn of my salvation, my stronghold.
– Psalm 18:2

THE STRONGHOLD

"Dad, the weatherman says a tornado might be coming," Riley said. "A tornado can blow our house away. Doesn't that scare you?"

"There's nothing to worry about, son," Mr. Carter said. He led Riley through the kitchen and down the steps into the basement. Mr. Carter opened a door to a small room. Shelves lined the walls, holding tools and boxes.

"Your work room," Riley said. "So what?"

"So this is our stronghold," Mr. Carter said. "If the storm gets scary, we'll come down here."

Riley entered the room. He knocked on a wall. "Concrete," he said.

"So is the ceiling," Mr. Carter pointed out. "We're underneath the side porch right now, under a heavy, solid concrete floor."

"No windows in here," Riley said. "So the storm can't get in."

"A tornado couldn't hurt us in here," his father assured him. "We're underground. We're surrounded by concrete. We're safe."

"Even if the house blew away?" Riley asked.

His dad nodded again. "Even if the house went flying like a kite, this room would still be here."

"What did you call it?" Riley asked.

A stronghold," Mr. Carter said. "A strong place that will hold us safely."

Riley studied the room.

"Tell you what," his father said. "We can come down here right now, if you like. You get the checker board and set it up on the work bench. I'll get a couple of chairs."

A few minutes later, as they played checkers, Riley said, "I like having a stronghold. I'm not scared any more."

"You should be," his father joked. "You should be scared of what I'm going to do to you on this checkerboard."

1. What is the safest place in your home?

PRAYER   God, I don't know what's coming, but I know You're my stronghold. Thanks! Amen.

ON A STORMY DAY

In Luke 8:22-25 there is a story about Jesus protecting the disciples on a dangerous day. Below, the story has gotten messed up and you'll have to fix it. Wherever you find the wrong word, scratch it out and add the right word. You can look the story up if you get stuck.

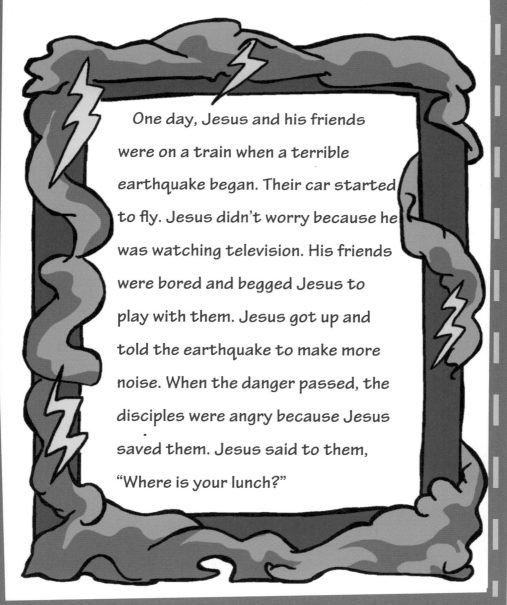

One day, Jesus and his friends were on a train when a terrible earthquake began. Their car started to fly. Jesus didn't worry because he was watching television. His friends were bored and begged Jesus to play with them. Jesus got up and told the earthquake to make more noise. When the danger passed, the disciples were angry because Jesus saved them. Jesus said to them, "Where is your lunch?"

GOD OF THE IMPOSSIBLE

There is nothing God cannot do.
What is impossible with men is possible with God.
– Luke 18:27

HEART TROUBLE

Nick sat in a bed wearing a hospital gown. A wall-mounted television was on, and a dinner tray sat beside the hospital bed.

Jose and Will walked into the room uncertainly.

"How's it going?" Will asked.

"I'm feeling fine," Nick said. "I'll be well before midterms."

"Then it's not too bad," Jose said. He sounded relieved.

"Oh, it's pretty bad," Nick said. "My heart is messed up. It's a problem I was born with. But I'm still getting well."

"This is a great hospital," Will said. "They took care of my grandfather here."

"Cable TV," Nick said. "Dinner in bed. And nurse Gwen is totally cute."

"Maybe we should come back when she's on duty," Jose said.

"Oh, Gwen," Will said, making kissing sounds.

"How about your doctor?" Jose asked.

"She's going to put a pig valve in my heart," Nick said. "Maybe I'll grow a curly tail and start oinking."

"That's too weird," Will said.

"But I'm still going to get well," Nick said, "even if they use a skunk valve."

He opened the drawer beside his bed and took out a Bible. He opened the book to a marked page and handed it to Jose.

"The part that's underlined," Nick said. "Read it out loud."

Jose said, "Matthew 19:26. 'With God all things are possible.'"

"So whatever is wrong with your heart, God can fix it if that is his plan for you," said Will.

"And why wouldn't he want to?" Nick asked. "After all, you guys will never pass math without me."

All three boys laughed.

"Your heart will be fine," Jose said, "if it doesn't get broken by nurse Gwen."

YOUR TURN

1. Just because God can do anything, does it mean God will say yes to everything we ask for? Why?

_____

PRAYER   God, remind me that what seems impossible to me is easy for You. Amen.

HOW HEALTHY ARE YOU?

God gives us lots of tools to get healthy and stay healthy. See if you can find the ones hidden in this word search. Some words are backwards and upside down. Can you think of other ways to take care of your health?

DOCTOR	DIET	SEAT BELT
HOSPITAL	FRIENDS	
MEDICINE	FAITH	
EXERCISE	SUNSCREEN	
SLEEP	BIKE HELMET	

```
Y B I K E H E L M E T W Q T E I D E Y T
E V X M Z N A S L K F P G H I I Q E H F
W U S D N E I R F B C N K D P H F J O B
J D I T O W H G A V Z N E X M E A N V T
E F R O F C W S G F Q R E E A S D H F L
H R E I T R T G H K F N C B R I E B B E
T D E O L T R O E W H G A H B C L H G B
I J P F K R H W R S J G K T V R S B D T
A E E N I C I D E M G F U O E E J N E A
F J E B C J A G S I P Q E H J X U R U E
H J L K H O S P I T A L Q G W E V B O S
A B S H S D G T R F S O U E Q B G J O B
```

■ FORGIVEN ■

When God forgives us, he no longer holds our sins against us.

For I will forgive their wickedness
and will remember their sins no more
– Hebrews 8:12

THE BIG JUMP

Colby flopped on the couch in his friend Phil's room. He said, "My sister has a broken arm because of me."

"Carla broke her arm?" Phil asked. "What happened?"

"There was a ladder propped up against the back of our house," Colby said. "I dared Carla to jump off the third step of the ladder. She did it and then dared me to jump off the fourth step."

"I can see where this is going," Phil said.

Colby nodded miserably. "She was pretty high up the ladder," he said.

"Then Carla took the big jump and ka-boom?" Phil guessed.

"I heard her arm crack when she fell," Colby told his friend. "Why was I so stupid?"

"How is Carla now?" Phil asked.

"Okay, I guess," Colby said. "She's got a cast, but she says it doesn't hurt too much. The doctor told us it was a clean break and will heal fine."

"Are your parents mad at you?" Phil asked.

"No, they've been really nice about it," Colby said.

"I'll bet Carla is ready to strangle you," Phil said.

Colby shook his head. "She let me be the first one to sign her cast," he said. "She says it was her own fault."

They sat in silence for a moment.

"I should never have started such a crazy game," Colby said.

"Okay, you did something dumb," Phil said, "but Carla's going to be okay. Get over it."

"It's not that easy," Colby said.

"Sure it is," Phil said. "You told Carla you're sorry. Now tell God you're sorry and move on. Trust me, Colby. If you'll forget about this, so will God."

YOUR TURN

1. Have you ever blamed yourself for something you did wrong?

_____

God, everybody messes up sometimes. Thanks for offering me forgiveness when I ask for it. Amen.

FORGIVEN, FORGOTTEN, AND FLUSHED

When we have trouble forgiving ourselves, we can remember that God always forgives us when we tell him we're sorry.

Here's something you can do to remind yourself that God is willing to forgive and forget our mistakes.

Take a tissue and write the word SIN on it. You'll need to write carefully so the tissue won't tear. Or, if you want, you can write on the tissue some things you want to tell God you're sorry about.

When you've finished writing on the tissue, hold it in your hand and say this prayer: "God, forgive my sins and help me forgive myself."

Now take the tissue and tear it into as many tiny pieces as you can. When you finish tearing it up, drop it in the toilet and flush it away.

When the pieces of tissue are gone, say thank you to God and feel His love filling you up.

FORGIVEN AND FORGIVING

God forgives us and expects us to forgive others.

For if you forgive men when they sin against you,
your heavenly Father will also forgive you.
– Matthew 6:14

OUT ON A LIMB

"I'm never talking to Brad again," Caleb said.

"Give me a leg up," Eric said, peering into the maple tree.

Eric stepped into Caleb's cupped hands and grabbed a limb. He swung into the tree.

Caleb tossed him one end of a thick rope. Eric stuck it in his belt and climbed higher. A cool breeze rolled from the lake and rustled the leaves.

"Brad got our lunch table in trouble," Caleb said. "Everybody got detention. I wasn't the one throwing butter into the air. I told Brad he should stop. Did he listen? No. He was determined to stick a pat of butter on the ceiling."

"Why did he want to do that?" Eric asked.

"Because he's nuttier than a jar of extra-crunchy," Caleb said.

"What about that time at lunch when you tried to eat the lima beans of everybody at the table?" Eric reminded him. "Remember you barfed green chunks all over the floor?"

"That was different," Caleb said. "I didn't cause problems for anyone else."

"You might want to ask the custodian about that," Eric said. "Look, everybody does goofy stuff sometimes. God forgives us. We forgive each other. We move on."

Eric edged along a tree limb hanging over the lake. "How's this?" he asked.

"Perfect," Caleb called.

Eric triple knotted the rope to the limb, yanked it a few times, then climbed slowly down the rope to the bank.

"This is gonna be so great," Caleb said. "We swing over the lake, let go, and splash!"

"Tomorrow after school, we try it out," Eric said.

"Maybe I'll invite Brad over, too," Caleb said.

Eric smiled. "Sounds good to me."

YOUR TURN

1. Is it hard for you to forgive the mistakes other people make?

_____

PRAYER God, I guess if You can forgive me, then I can forgive others. At least, I can try. Amen.

LEARNING TO FORGIVE

If only we had a DELETE button for some of the dumb and mean things we say to each other. In these comic strips, there are some words that need deleting. In each cartoon, the second person says something that makes things worse. Try writing different words in the third panel to make a better ending.

TURNING IT OVER

God helps us carry the heavy stuff in life.

Cast your cares on the LORD and he will sustain you.
– Psalm 55:22

WORRYING ABOUT WAYNE

Chase set his tray on the table and said, "You know that guy Wayne, the one my mom has been dating?"

"Sure," Adam said. "He's always telling your mom she's too easy on you, that you need more discipline, he wouldn't let you get away with so much, blah-blah-blah."

"He proposed to Mom yesterday," Chase said. "I'm praying a lot."

"Praying for your mom not to marry Wayne?" Adam asked.

"I might have mentioned that to God," Chase said, grinning. "Mostly I'm asking God to settle me down and help me through whatever comes."

Adam nodded.

"Maybe your mom will decide Wayne isn't the right guy," he said.

"Or maybe Wayne will ease up on me," Chase suggested. "Or I might learn to like him more. I'm sure God has a plan."

Chase took a bite of mac and cheese and washed it down with milk.

"Talking to God about it makes me feel better," Chase said.

"Really?" Adam asked. "I don't pray much. How does it work?"

Chase shrugged.

"I don't think I can explain it exactly," he said. "At first, I'm all upset and I tell God how awful everything is. You know, how Wayne bugs me, and how I wish it would just be Mom and me like it always has been. I pour it all out to God. I guess I kind of throw my junk on God and let him carry it. After a while I feel calmer."

"Peaceful?" Adam asked.

"Yeah," Chase said. "Just knowing that God cares and understands, makes me feel warm inside. Does that sound dorky?"

"It sounds great," Adam told him. "I think I'll try it."

YOUR TURN

1. Does telling God your problems make you feel better?

_____

_____

PRAYER

God, when things are weighing me down, can I turn them over to You? Would You carry them for me? Amen.

TWO THINGS

You don't have to carry your problems by yourself. There are two things you can always turn over to God and ask him to carry them for you. To find out which two things, use the clues to find the letter that goes in each blank.

_____ THE BEST GRADE YOU CAN GET

_____ THE OPPOSITE OF OUT

_____ THIS LETTER IS A QUESTION

_____ SOMETHING YOU CAN DRINK HOT OR COLD

_____ LOOKS LIKE A FOOTBALL GOAL POST

_____ DO YOU HAVE TWO OF THESE IN YOUR FACE?

_____ A Z KNOCKED ON ITS SIDE

_____ THE SEVENTH LETTER IN THE ALPHABET

AND

_____ A BACKWARDS 3

_____ LOOKS LIKE A TWO-FINGER PEACE SIGN

_____ ANOTHER BACKWARDS 3

_____ "I AM. HE IS. THEY _____ ."

_____ POR QUE?

_____ SOMETHING TO SET A GOLF BALL ON

_____ THE LETTER YOU CAN'T HEAR IN "HONEST"

_____ "ME, MYSELF, AND _____ ."

_____ THIS LETTER IS ALMOST AN M

_____ THE FIRST OR LAST SYLLABLE OF GEOLOGY

CHAPTER SIX

THREE
SIXTY-FIVE

TALKING TO GOD

We can talk to God every day.

Devote yourselves to prayer, being watchful and thankful.

– Colossians 4:2

STARTING THE NEW YEAR RIGHT

Dear God,

It's January 1, the beginning of a brand new year. I've figured out what I'm going to do to celebrate the new year. I'm going to pray every day. My Sunday school teacher says that there are lots of ways to pray besides talking to You in my head. Singing Christian songs is praying. One time King David danced his prayer to You. I wish I could have seen that prayer!

Some people even write their prayers. There's a whole book of written prayers in the Bible. It's called Psalms, but I guess You already know that, right? Anyway, I'm going to try writing a prayer to You every day this year. That's scary! Three hundred sixty-five prayers! On nights when I have a bunch of homework, it might be a short prayer. But I'm not going to miss a single day. Not one!

I'm not sure what I'll talk about, but I guess I'll tell You what's going on in my life, how things are going, that sort of stuff. Sometimes the things I do don't seem very interesting or exciting. Do You like to hear from me even when I'm not doing anything big?

I'm going to start reading the Bible, too. That should give me more things to write about. In my prayers I'm talking to You, and in the Bible You're talking to me. That's totally cool! It's like we're pen-pals.

Okay, it's time for me to go to bed. I was up late last night to hear the sirens and see the fireworks at midnight. I'll write to You tomorrow, God. Thanks for reading this.

YOUR TURN

1. How often do you talk to God? Is it every day?

_____

2. If God already knows everything, why do we tell God things?

_____

God, You love me so much that it makes You happy when I take time to talk to You. I'm going to try to talk to You more, but if I forget sometimes I know You'll still love me. Amen.

ONE WAY TO PRAY

There are many ways to pray to God. If you have trouble thinking of things to say to God, here is one way you might like to pray.

First, tell God how wonderful He is.

Second, tell God you're sorry for your mistakes and sins.

Third, thank God for the good things in your life.

Fourth, ask for God's help for others and for yourself.

You can spend as much time on each one as you want. Even if you only pray for a minute or two, God loves to hear from you.

Try writing a prayer below by finishing each of the sentences. When you're done, you can read it aloud to God.

ONE OF A KIND

God made you and nobody else is exactly like you.

The Spirit of God has made me;
the breath of the Almighty gives me life.
– Job 33:4

SNOW DAY

January 17

Yay, God! There must be a foot of snow on the ground, and it's still coming down. The snow is so thick in the air, I can hardly see across the street. This is going to be the best day of all time: sledding, snowball fights, and a giant snowman in the front yard.

Mom says that no two snowflakes are alike. Is that true? It looks like there are a jillion snowflakes in our yard. Did You make every one different from all the others? How can You think up so many different shapes? It seems like a lot of trouble just for snow. In a few days all this will be gone, melted away. The next time it snows, You'll have to make another jillion snowflakes—all different! Wow!

If You work so hard to make each snowflake special, You must work even harder to make each person special. Did You have fun planning me? You picked out the color for my eyes and hair. You figured out how tall I'd be and whether I'd be left-handed or right-handed. I'm not wild about my freckles, but I guess You must like them. You decided I'd be good in language arts, and You put that birthmark on my belly—the one shaped like a lima bean. In the whole world, I'm the only me.

Since You went to so much trouble making me, I must be special to You. I'm glad You make every snowflake and every person different. The way You create things is so awesome. You really did a great job on me. Wait until You see the snowman I'm going to make!

YOUR TURN

1. What things about you make you different from your friends?

_____

2. Why do you think God made so many different kinds of plants and animals and people?

_____

PRAYER God, thank You for making me who I am. There's nobody else exactly like me. Thanks to You, I am one of a kind! Amen.

NO ONE LIKE ME

There is no one exactly like you, and here's a diagram to show some ways you are special. First, write your name in one of the circles. Put the names of two other people you know in the other two circles. Write the things in each circle that describes each person. In the middle over-lapping section, write some of the things that you all have in common. Below are some ideas to get you started.

Can climb a tree
Knows lots of words
Is a good reader
Likes frozen yogurt
Is good at working with little children
Likes to help older people
Is generous

Is good with computers
Can write songs
Is a good cook
Can make a Powerpoint presentation
Has curly hair
Is good at sports

GOD OF TOMORROW

Whatever happens in the future, God will watch over us.

Even to your old age and gray hairs I am he, I am he who will sustain you. I have made you and I will carry you.
— Isaiah 46:4

THE GROUNDHOG'S SHADOW

February 2

God, this has to be the dumbest day on the calendar. Somewhere in Pennsylvania, a groundhog comes out of his hole today. If he sees his shadow, it means we will have six more weeks of winter. If he doesn't see his shadow, then spring is almost here. How can a groundhog tell the future? Dumb with a capital D, almost as dumb as people who try to tell the future by watching stars or looking at somebody's palm. Duh! That's like flipping a coin to figure out the answers on a True-False test.

God, somebody needs to tell those groundhog watchers and fortune tellers that You are in charge of the future. You are the only one who can decide when winter is over and when the next season begins. You made the world, and You are the boss of everything in creation.

Sure, sometimes I'd like to peek into the future. I'd love to know how a ball game will turn out before it happens. When a comic book ends with Batman in a crashing helicopter, I hate waiting a whole month to find out how he's going to escape. It would be great to know what day it's going to rain before we plan a family camping trip. But we're just people and You're God, so You're always going to know more than we do. I trust You to make things turn out the way they should.

By the way, I don't believe in the groundhog weatherman, but I am getting tired of winter. The snow is fun, but I want to play baseball. Whether the little furry guy sees his shadow or not, I hope You'll bring spring soon.

YOUR TURN

1. Do you ever wonder what's going to happen in the future?

2. How do you feel knowing that God is in charge of the future? Do you think God will take care of everything?

PRAYER God, I'm going to do my best today, and I'll let You take care of tomorrow. Okay?

WE DON'T HAVE TO WORRY

The Bible tells us we don't have to worry about the future because we can always count on Jesus. Crack the code to complete the promise found in Hebrews 13:8.

February

		Mark out all the B's		Change the C's to D's
Mark out all the G's	Change the P's to O's		Mark out all the X's	Change the Z's to Y's	
	Mark out all the Q's	Change the K's to T's			Mark out all the M's
		Change the N's to R's		

BBZBGXQMEQGMSBBKGXEMMGNQQXCQBAGXXQZ

BKGQQMPBXCAQZM

BBMFXQBBGPMGMGNXXQEMBGVGGBEQXNMMB

Jesus Christ is the same ＿＿＿＿＿＿＿ and

＿＿＿＿＿＿＿ and ＿＿＿＿＿＿＿.

■ MORE THAN HEARTS AND MUSH ■

Jesus wants us to love each other in the same way He loves us.

As I have loved you, so you must love one another.
— **John 13:34**

THE DANCE

February 14

God, Seth wanted to go to the Valentine's Day dance after school today, so I went for a while and hung with him. The disc jockey was pretty good. So was the food. Mostly the girls bunched up on one side of the gym and the boys on the other. There wasn't much dancing, just girls dancing with other girls.

Madeline came up to me while I was at the food table. She asked me if I wanted to dance. My face got hot and I must have turned as red as the heart cupcakes. I told her I wasn't a dancer, but thanks anyway.

I guess Seth saw what happened. He made kissy sounds as we walked home and asked me where we were going to have the wedding. If Seth wasn't my best friend, I'd buy him a one-way ticket to the North Pole.

God, I'm not sure I understand this love stuff. Mom and Dad love each other. I get that. But girls are just weird. Everybody says I'll change my mind about girls one day. I guess so, but love is bigger than just boys and girls, right? Love is for parents, too, isn't it? And brothers and best friends and pets and even favorite teachers. If we're supposed to love everybody, love must be more than hearts and mushy stuff. Maybe love is how we treat people—being good to each other, helping, showing we care. If that's what love is, I can do that. If it means dancing with girls, I'm not so sure.

Madeline is kind of cute, but don't tell anybody I said so.

1. What does it mean to love somebody?

_____

2. How do you treat someone when you love them? Can you give some examples of how you treat the people you love?

_____

God, loving everybody the way Jesus loves sounds pretty hard. Maybe I can start with the people in my own house and go from there. Amen.

WHAT DOES LOVE LOOK LIKE?

The Bible tells us how to love God and how to love one another. Find out how by discovering the message from Mark 12:30-31 hidden in the wheels. Start with the circled letter and skip the second letter. Read the third and skip the fourth. Go around the circle twice and write your answer in the spaces next to the cupcake. Then do the same thing with the second wheel.

Fill in the blanks:

(Wheel 1 letters: G R O T D A W N I D T S H O A U L L A Y O D O U M R I H N E D A)

Love the Lord your ___ ___ ___

___ ___ ___ ___   ___ ___ ___   ___

___ ___ ___   ___ ___ ___ ___ ___

___ ___ ___ ___ ___ ___ ___

___ ___ ___

___ ___ ___ ___ ___   ___ ___ ___ ___

___ ___ ___

___ ___ ___

___

___ ___   ___ ___ ___ ___ ___

(Wheel 2 letters: A H N B D O L R O A V S E Y Y O O U R R S N E E L I F G)

DRESSED IN CHRIST

God's forgiveness washes us clean of sin.

For all of you who were baptized into Christ have clothed yourselves with Christ.

– Galatians 3:27

SPRING CLEANING

March 16

Ugh! Mom is doing spring cleaning, God. She goes through the whole house with buckets, mops, and scrub brushes. The furniture gets moved around, the sweeper runs all day, and every room smells like soap. Yesterday I cleaned the windows—every window, inside and out. If I left any streaks, Mom made me do it over. I used enough paper towels to build a tent.

Today Mom gave me a bucket of paint, a brush, and a roller. She told me not to come out of my room until I had painted the walls. It's a good thing Mom covered the floor with old sheets, or I would have accidentally painted the carpet, too.

Once I got started, the painting was fun. The new color wasn't much different from the old color, but the fresh paint was so pure and clean. My walls were pretty dirty. There were tape marks from posters and black scuffs from that sleepover when Seth and I had the shoe-throwing fight. Oh, yeah, and there was a real ugly spot where I bounce the volleyball off the wall while I lie in bed.

Even though it was hard work, the room looked brighter when the new paint went on. I liked rolling the fresh paint over the old ugly paint, covering it over and making it disappear.

It made me think of something I read in the Bible about dressing myself in Christ. I must be like those dirty walls, scuffed up and dirty from the bad things I've done. When You wrap me up in Jesus, His goodness covers over my mistakes like a fresh coat of paint. Thanks for Your spring cleaning, God.

YOUR TURN

1. Can you think of something you've done that bothers you? Have you asked God to forgive you?

   _____

2. How does it make you feel to know that you are wrapped in the goodness and love of Jesus?

   _____

PRAYER God, I mess up sometimes. Well, actually, I mess up a lot. Thanks for forgiving me. I'll try to do better next time. Amen.

CLEANING THINGS UP

Dressing in Christ means replacing old ways of thinking and acting with new ways. Read the words in the articles of clothing below. If dressing in Christ means replacing this way of thinking or acting, cross out the word and write in the best way to replace it.

OUT OF THE GRAVE

Jesus died for us, but God has raised him from the dead.
*But God raised him from the dead, freeing him
from the agony of death, because it was impossible
for death to keep its hold on him.*

– Acts 2:24

A ROLLING STONE

Easter Sunday

Wow, God! You did a great job making this day. The sun is shining. There are flowers in the yard and on the dogwood trees. On the way home from church we rolled the car windows down. I heard birds singing and smelled wild onions. What a beautiful spring.

But the best part of today is that it's Easter. This morning, the preacher talked about Jesus coming out of the tomb. He said it was a little like a butterfly coming out of the cocoon. The caterpillar makes a cocoon, crawls inside, and waits in the dark. Then when nobody's expecting it, a butterfly climbs out of the cocoon. That's the way it was for Jesus. After He was hung on the cross, they put His body inside a stone tomb and closed it up. For a while He stayed there in the dark, but on Easter He rolled back the stone from the tomb and came back alive into the world. Nobody was ready for that! The Roman soldiers at the grave were so afraid that they fainted.

Jesus' friends must have been so happy to see him alive again. It makes me happy, too. That big rock that sealed the tomb couldn't keep Jesus from coming to His friends. There's nothing that can keep Jesus from coming to be with me, either. He is stronger than the Roman guards, stronger than a huge rock, even stronger than death. As long as Jesus is with me, there's nothing for me ever to be afraid of. I've got the strongest one in the universe on my side.

Happy Easter, God. You're the best!

YOUR TURN

1. How does it make you feel that Jesus came back from the dead? If He had stayed in the grave, would it make any difference to you?

_____

2. If Jesus could beat death, do you think there is anything in this world that is stronger than Him?

_____

PRAYER   Jesus, I'm amazed that You died for me and then came back from the dead. You are the Lord! Amen.

Easter Surprise

Look at the two pictures and circle 7 things in the second picture that are different from the first picture.

NEVER ALONE

God helps us through tough days.

Cast all your anxiety on him because he cares for you.
– I Peter 5:7

THE AWFUL DAY

March 29

God, this has been a lousy day.

I overslept this morning and missed the school bus, so I had to walk to school in the rain. My shoes were soaked when I got there and my feet were icicles. I caught a cold and sneezed all day. Since I was late to school, I had to go to the principal's office. When I got to class, I realized I'd left my math assignment at home. Even though I did the work, Mrs. Taylor gave me a zero.

After the last bell, I remembered that I had left my history book in science class. Even though I went to get my book at super-speed, I missed the bus AGAIN! I had to walk home, and it was still raining. Every time a car passed me, the tires splashed water on me. When I got home, I was wet and filthy. When I tried to dry off, I got dirt on one of the good towels and Mom yelled at me for messing up the towel and dripping water on the living room carpet.

For dinner we had liver—the nastiest food in the world. When I didn't eat any yucky liver, Mom yelled some more. God, if You're thinking about adding any new commandments, Number Eleven should be, "Thou shalt never, ever cook liver."

After dinner, the rain turned into a big storm and the power went out. No electricity means no TV, and I missed Superville, my favorite show. I'm using a flashlight to write this prayer. The only good thing about this day is that I know You've been beside me all day.

Thanks for hanging with me. Please make tomorrow better.

YOUR TURN

1. Do you think it's easier to handle a bad day if you remember that God is with you? Why do you think that?

_____

2. How does God respond when you're having a hard time?

_____

PRAYER Lord, thanks for being with me all the time. When everything is going great, I love to share it with You. And when everything is awful, it makes me feel better that You're with me. Amen.

GOD WAS THERE...

For all the good days and the bad days of your life, God has been with you. Draw pictures of things that have happened to you and remember how you knew God was there.

The day you were born.

When you got sick or hurt.

When you had a great day at school.

When something awesome happened.

▬ BEING A FRIEND ▬

God wants us to give help to each other.

*Carry each other's burdens, and in this way
you will fulfill the law of Christ.*

— **Galatians 6:2**

THE TALL GRASS

May 14

God, I got sort of mad at Seth today. All week we've been planning to go the movies today. When I called Seth this morning to see whether we were seeing the 1:00 movie or the 3:30 showing, he said he might not be able to go. He had to cut the grass before he could go anywhere. Seth has this huge yard, and it takes a long time to mow it and do all the trimming.

I could hardly believe he was messing up our plans. Why didn't he cut the grass yesterday or the day before? Didn't he know he was letting me down? After all, we'd made plans together.

Then I remembered that Seth had been super busy on a science fair project all week. Also, it had rained for the last three days. Seth couldn't mow his lawn while the rain was falling. This problem wasn't his fault.

Instead of being mad, I decided to help. I rode my bicycle to Seth's house. While Seth ran the lawnmower, I trimmed around the trees, bushes, and his mother's flower garden. The grass was really tall, so when he finished cutting, we both raked up the clippings. After we carried the grass to the compost, Seth swept the drive while I cleaned off the sidewalk.

Working together, the job didn't take so long. Seth's mother said we did such a good job that we deserved a reward, and she gave us money for popcorn at the theater. I felt good knowing I had helped Seth, and the movie was more fun with my best friend than it would have been alone.

God, I'm so glad I'm not alone in the world.

YOUR TURN

1. Do you have a friend you would help out? Would your friend do the same thing for you?

_____

2. If you were the person in the story, would you have helped Seth mow his lawn or would you have gone to the movie alone?

_____

PRAYER

God, thanks for friends and people who give me help when I need it. Amen.

BETTER DONE WITH A FRIEND

Look at the pictures below and decide which activities would be better if a friend were helping you. For the activities that would be better with a friend, write a few words or a sentence telling how your friend would make it better. For the activities you'd rather do alone, write a sentence telling why you don't need a friend.

THE FOREVER GOD
God has always been and will always be.

*Do not forsake me, O God, till I declare your power
to the next generation, your might to all who are to come.*
– Psalm 71:18

THE BEST BIRTHDAY PRESENT

July 16

Happy birthday to me, God! I love my birthday. Mom will bake me a cake,
and we'll have chocolate chip ice cream with sprinkles. Double yum! My
friend Seth is coming over for dinner. I get presents, too. I hope I get that
video game I've been dropping hints for a month about. I wish I could have
more than one a year. Birthdays should come every month.

Gosh, I guess You never have a birthday party, do You, God? I know Jesus
does—that's Christmas—but You don't have a birthday, because You were
never born. Is that right? I know You made everything, but when I was a kid
I thought maybe somebody made You. I asked Dad about that, and he smiled.
He said he used to wonder the same thing. Then he told me that nobody made
You. There was never a time before You. Everything else was made, but You
are the Maker. Before there was a world or a universe, You were already there.

Trying to figure this out makes my head hurt! This is harder than math.
But I like knowing that You are forever. You never die or get old or go away.
You are my God for always and always, no matter what. Someday I'll have
a birthday when I'm old and gray. My grandkids will be there. I'll have to
wear glasses to see the cake, and I won't have enough wind to blow out eighty
candles. But You won't be any older. You'll still be the same, and You will
still be taking care of me.

That is the best birthday present of all!

YOUR TURN

1. Besides God, can you think of anything that lasts forever?

_____

2. Who is the oldest person you know? What do think it will feel like
when you are that old?

_____

PRAYER   God, no matter how many years go by, You will always be
my God. Amen.

BIRTHDAY PARTY FOR GOD

If you were having a birthday party for God, what do you think the best gifts would be? Mark out the things that you think would NOT be good gifts for God. Then choose one gift, or make up your own, and make a promise to give that gift.

Riding my bike to my friend's house instead of asking someone to drive me in a car.

Helping my little brother or sister with chores.

Breaking off tree branches on a hiking trail.

Helping plant flowers or trees in the park.

Collecting cans for re-cycling.

Throwing garbage in the bushes behind the school.

Turning off the lights when I leave the room to save energy.

Singing in the youth choir at church

TOUGH ENOUGH

When things get tough, we can keep trying.

Nevertheless, the righteous will hold to their ways.

– Job 17:9

NO QUITTER

September 28

God, I bombed on the math test today. There were a bunch of problems I didn't know how to solve. Who cares how long the shadow is on a thirty-foot flagpole at three o'clock? Time ran out and I didn't even get to the end of the test. I can already picture that big, fat "F" in red ink.

Dad's going to be mad. He thinks I'm not trying, but I studied for hours last night. It's not fair. I get good grades in my other subjects. Remember that "A" on my history report last week? And the "B+" on the science quiz? But I just can't figure out this math stuff.

Why was math ever invented? I worked hard to get ready for this test, and I still did a lousy job. I feel like quitting. I might as well let Mrs. Taylor flunk me, and I'll take the class again in summer school.

I don't want to be a quitter. I know quitters never get anywhere. There must have been times when Jesus got discouraged, too. When people wouldn't listen to him, when His friends let him down, when Peter wouldn't stand up for Him, I'll bet Jesus felt like quitting. But he didn't give up. He kept doing His best no matter what.

Someday I won't have to take any more math classes, but for now I guess I'll keep doing my best. I know that's what You want me to do. I might never be good at math, but at least I'll keep trying.

And God, if You want to give me a passing grade on that test, it's totally okay with me.

YOUR TURN

1. Have you ever wanted to give up, but you kept trying anyway? How do you feel about that now?

_____

2. When you see athletes or musicians on TV, do you think any of them were quitters? Why do you think that?

_____

God, I know I can't be good at everything. Help me know which things I should keep working on and which ones are a waste of time. Amen.ones are a waste of time. Amen.

KEEP GOING

Lots of times it would be easier to give up and quit than to keep on trying, but quitting gets you nowhere. Here is a list of things that you have to keep working on if you want to succeed. Add some ideas of your own (or ask a parent for ideas). Then write down some things you might say to a friend who wants to quit. Who knows? You might need to say them to yourself one day.

- **Becoming a great chess player**

- **Becoming a gymnast**

- **Learning to play a musical instrument**

- **Making the Honor Roll**

- **Skateboarding**

_____

_____

_____

_____

If my friend wanted to give up and quit trying, I would tell him:

_____

_____

_____

_____

SAD DAYS

> **Crying is nothing to be ashamed of.**
> *Jesus wept.*
> — John 11:35

MISSING MY BUDDY

October 4

God, I started crying in school today. I saw a picture of a dog in our social studies book, and it reminded me of Duke. I told You about my dog Duke last week. He'd been my friend since I was born. Duke finally got too old to run with me. He was nearly blind and couldn't climb up and down the steps anymore. When he died, it was the saddest day I can ever remember. I cried all day. Even Dad cried a little when we took Duke out into the woods to bury him.

Most of the time I can remember Duke and not be sad, but the dog in the picture I saw at school looked just like my little buddy. All of a sudden I missed him so much. Mrs. Higdon didn't notice me crying, but a bunch of kids did. I hate letting people see me cry. It makes me feel like a sissy, but I know that can't be right. Jesus cried sometimes, and He was a real man, not a sissy. You have to be pretty tough to hang on a cross!

Why did You invent tears, God? Maybe when we're full of feelings, tears keep us from bursting. I don't like to feel bad, but it doesn't mean anything is wrong with me. Everybody gets sad. Jesus was sad when His friend Lazarus died. He was so sad, He cried in front of a whole crowd of people.

I still don't want a bunch of friends to see me cry, but I guess crying can't be so bad or You wouldn't have built us this way. God, thanks for being with me on this sad day.

YOUR TURN

1. Do you try to make sure nobody sees you when you cry? Why?

_____

_____

2. How would you feel about a friend if you saw him crying?

_____

PRAYER

God, please love me on the glad days and the sad days and the in-between days. Amen.

EVERY TEAR

Nobody wants to be a cry-baby, but everybody cries sometimes—boys and girls, kids and grown-ups—everybody! Just remember that even if nobody else sees you cry, God sees and cares. In a prayer from the Psalms, a sad person says to God, "Put my tears in your bottle." Every tear is precious to God, and he understands our sadness.

In the teardrops below, write some things that have made you sad—maybe some things that still make you sad. As you write them down, give them to God.

■ RAINED OUT ■

God provides water and food for everyone.

He bestows rain on the earth;
he sends water upon the countryside.
– Job 5:10

THE MUDDY MAZE

October 23

God, my church youth group was supposed to go to the corn maze today. Acres and acres of cornfields with paths and dead ends like a giant puzzle. The first member of the youth group to reach the flag in the middle would get a chocolate milkshake on the way home. I've always wanted to go and this was the big day. So here's my question, God: Why did You rain out the church trip to the maze? Didn't You want me to go?

You didn't just send a sprinkle of rain. No, You made roof-pounding rain, the kind that fills the ditches and washes the gutters. Hours of rain. It started before I got up and it's still going. Mr. Bretz just phoned to tell me that the trip is called off. It's so muddy at the corn maze that they've closed it for a few days.

You've ruined my day so You can turn the rain off now. Thanks for messing up the trip. Why didn't You send the rain tomorrow? Why did it have to be today? Don't You care about me at all?

Okay, I'm sorry I said that. I know I'm being dumb. No matter what day You send the rain, it's going to wreck somebody's picnic or playoff game or hike. I know we need rain to grow crops and to keep water running through the faucet. Come to think of it, if You didn't send rain, there wouldn't even be a corn maze.

Mr. Bretz said we'd try to visit the maze next Saturday. I hope we'll have a sunny day, but whatever You decide is okay with me. You know what's best.

1. Do you think God cares about your happiness?

_____

2. Would you want the job of taking care of all the people and animals in the world? Why?

_____

PRAYER God, I don't always understand why You do the things You do, but I trust You to do what's right. I'm glad You're in charge instead of me. Amen.

JESUS KNOWS HOW YOU FEEL

People have lots of different feelings and emotions. Bible stories tell us that Jesus experienced all the feelings we have, so Jesus knows how we feel all the time. How do you think Jesus felt in each of the following situations?

• Jesus visited his friends Lazarus, Mary and Martha for dinner.

    I think Jesus felt _____.

    I feel this way when _____

    _____.

• Jesus had been preaching all day and he was tired, but people kept coming to him and asking for his help.

    I think Jesus felt _____

    _____.

    I feel this way when _____

    _____.

• Jesus went to the Temple and found people stealing and lying instead of praying and worshiping God.

    I think Jesus felt _____.

    I feel this way when _____.

• Jesus was arrested and his good friend, Peter, said that he did not know who Jesus was.

    I think Jesus felt _____.

    I feel this way when _____.

• Jesus was preaching so long that it was lunchtime and no one knew where they would get food. Then, someone found a boy with some bread and fish and the boy was willing to share with others.

    I think Jesus felt _____.

    I feel this way when _____.

Does it help you to know Jesus understands your feelings?

THANKING GOD

We give thanks because every good thing comes from God.
O Lord my God, I will give you thanks forever.
– Psalm 30:12

THE ABC'S OF THANKSGIVING

November 26

God, I know this going to sound weird, but in English class today I started thinking about how cool my hand is. The way my fingers work lets me do a bazillion things—write my name, scratch my back, pull out splinters, wave goodbye, swing a bat, play rock-paper-scissors, shuffle cards, type on the computer, and more things than I can even think of. I don't think I've ever thanked You for my hands. So thanks! They're totally awesome.

There must be lots of things I've never thanked You for. I think I'll try to make a list using every letter of the alphabet. Here goes: Thank You, God, for apple pie, banana splits, camping trips, digital cameras, electricity, Florida (where we went on vacation last year), grass, hospitals, ice cream, Jaguars (the cool cars, not the jungle cats), kites, libraries, monster movies, nature, omelets, penguins, quilts, root beer floats, swimming pools, turtles, underwear, volleyball, wool sweaters, X-Men comics, yoyos, and zoos.

Gosh, that was easy. I think I'll do it again. Thank You, God for airplanes, beds, chocolate cake, dogs, extra-credit questions, falling stars, gravity, hair, Iron Man, jokes, koala bears, lemonade, music, nachos, oxygen, pizza, quacking ducks, radio stations, sleep, teeth, umbrellas, video games, waterfalls, x-rays, YouTube, and zippers.

This is really easy. If it weren't for Q and X, I could do this all day and never run out of blessings. Even if I used a calculator, I couldn't count all the good things You give me. I guess You do all these wonderful things for me just because You love me. You're the best!

YOUR TURN

1. When you think about this day, what things make you thankful?

_____

2. Do you say thank you to God before each meal? Do you think that is enough thanksgiving?

_____

PRAYER God, I could never list all the things You do for me. So I'll just say thanks for everything. Amen.

AS EASY AS ABC

Are you feeling creative? Great! You get to dream up your own prayer of thanksgiving. But instead of doing the whole alphabet, you can use the letters in your name to make your very own one-of-a-kind prayer to God. Write the letters of your name down the left side of the page, then for each letter think of something you are thankful for. You can write that word beside the letter (or draw it, if that's more fun.) When your name prayer is finished, maybe you can pray it with your family.

God, thank you for...

EVERY DAY WITH SUNSHINE
When we reach out for God, he reaches out for us.
Come near to God and he will come near to you.
– James 4:8

DAY 365
December 31

I did it, God. It's been a whole year, and I've written a prayer to You every day. Sometimes, I was so busy that I almost forgot. There were days when I was tired and I thought maybe it would be okay if I skipped just one prayer. But I made a commitment and I kept it up.

I feel like You and I know each other better after all these prayers. Of course, You've always known me. But I feel closer to You than I did before. The more time I spend with You, the more time I want to spend with You.

Now I know prayer works both ways. I talk to You and You talk to me. I've never heard Your voice in the air, but once in a while I get a feeling that You want me to do something. When I'm not sure about things, sometimes I can tell which choice You want me to make. That is so cool!

Spending time with You is making me a better person. I still lose my temper, but not as much as I used to. Is that because You're helping me? I think so. And I'm nicer to people since I started praying every day. Is that because Your love is getting into me? I hope so. Praying is like planting a flower in the sunshine. The more light shines on the flower, the bigger it grows. You're my sunshine, God. The more time I spend with You, the more I grow.

Let's make a deal. You keep shining, and I'll keep praying. I want to soak up Your love as long as I live.

YOUR TURN

1. Do you think you could talk to God every day this week? Will you try it?

_____

2. Do you feel close to God? Can you think of things that might make you feel closer?

_____

PRAYER
God, You always have time for me. I'm going to make sure that I always have time for You, too. Amen.

LOOKING BACK AT THE YEAR

For each panel, finish the caption and then draw a picture that shows an event that happened in the past year.

My family couldn't wait to
_____.

It was a lot of fun when
_____.

I couldn't believe my
parents heard about
_____.

I thought _____
_____ was
going to be a disaster, but
it turned out OK.

CHAPTER SEVEN

HOLY HEROES

HEROES IN STREET CLOTHES

It takes more than super powers to be a hero.

Imitate those who through faith and patience inherit what has been promised.

– Hebrews 6:12

THE SCHOOL PROJECT

Joel was excited as he got into the car.

"In computer lab, we get to do a research project on any subject we like," Joel told his dad.

"And you're going to research superheroes," his dad said with a smile.

"Yeah," Joel said. "Won't that be great?"

His dad said, "You won't learn much."

"But I love superheroes," Joel said.

His dad laughed.

"I love superheroes, too, but I'd like to see you stretch yourself," his dad said. "Why not do a project on real-life heroes? Spider-Man will never teach you how to walk on the ceiling, but studying some real heroes might teach you how to live."

The car came to a stop at a red light.

"No capes. No superpowers. No hidden caves," Joel complained. "Real life heroes just aren't as cool as superheroes."

The light turned green, but Joel's dad kept his foot on the brake.

"How come we're not going?" Joel asked.

"Take a look," his dad said.

A woman struggled to cross the highway. She leaned heavily on a walker. As she moved forward slowly, her limbs trembled and shook. She had started across the street while the light was red, but she moved so slowly that she couldn't make it to the other side before it turned green again.

Joel thought about how easy it was for him to walk and run, how well his own body worked. He watched the jerky movements of the woman as she inched across the pavement, forcing her feet to shuffle forward.

Without looking at Joel, his dad said, "She doesn't wear a cape."

"She doesn't need one," Joel decided. "She's already a hero."

YOUR TURN

1. What do you think makes a hero?

_____

PRAYER God, thanks for putting so many heroes in the world. I hope I can be a real-life hero, too. Amen.

MY HEROES

Fill in the blanks with the name of people in your life.
Then draw a picture of one or two of them as heroes.

_____ makes my life easier.

_____ is kind to people he/she doesn't know.

_____ takes good care of the earth.

_____ helps people who don't have necessary things.

_____ teaches me things.

_____ loves me no matter what I do.

STANDING UP FOR FRIENDS

God wants us to be kind to people who come from other lands.

When an alien lives with you in your land, do not mistreat him.
– Leviticus 19:33

SUPER KYLE

Joel settled his lunch tray on the table, nodding to Jorge and Kyle.

"I'm working on a class project about ordinary people who do heroic things," Joel said, sliding a straw into his milk. "Know any heroes I can write about?"

Jorge smiled and said, "Sí. He's sitting next to me."

Kyle bumped his shoulder and said, "Knock it off."

"Es la verdad," Jorge said, "Kyle is a hero to me."

"Did he save you from falling over a cliff or something?" Joel asked.

"When my family came from El Salvador," Jorge said, "it was hard. Everything was different in this country."

"When you started in this school, your English wasn't good," Joel said. "I'm almost flunking Social Studies in English. I don't think I could do it in another language."

Jorge nodded. "I'm not stupid, but I felt that way. Not everyone was kind to us. Because I look different, some people picked on me. One day a boy knocked my books from my hands. When I bent down to pick them up, he kicked the books across the hall."

"It was that troublemaker Jesse," Kyle said. "It really made me angry, so I helped Jorge pick up his books."

"Kyle didn't even know me," Jorge said. "But we became friends that day."

"No big deal," Kyle said. "Anybody would have helped."

Jorge shook his head. "Many watched and laughed. Only you helped."

Joel made notes on his napkin and shoved it in his pocket. He pulled a camera from his backpack. "Kyle, can I take your picture for my report?"

"I'm not a hero," Kyle insisted.

Joel took his picture anyway.

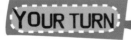

1. Why do you think people who look or speak differently get picked on?

_____

_____

God, You made every one of us. Show us how to get along with each other and to enjoy the things that make us different. Amen.

GOD'S PUZZLE

There is no one else exactly like you. God has made you special. God gives each of us special interests and abilities. Then, God helps us all live together like a pieces of a puzzle all fit together to form a picture.

Directions: Put your name on one of the puzzle pieces. Then, put the names of 4 friends or family members on the other puzzle pieces. Beside each of your friend's names, write or draw a picture of some way they are different from you. It may be a difference in the way you look or the things you like to play, your favorite subject in school or the make-up of your family, your favorite kind of pizza, or the kind of chores you prefer. Then, answer the following question:

Why do you think it is good that we are all a little bit different?

WELCOMING STRANGERS

God is glad when we share our time to help other people.
I was a stranger and you invited me in.
– Matthew 25:35

EXTRA STRONG LOVE

Joel hung around after basketball practice waiting for Jorge.

"Are you ready to meet some heroes?" Jorge asked, coasting up on his bike.

"You bet," Joel said.

The boys entered the school and walked to the cafeteria. Joel saw a dozen adults at the scattered tables, most of them in pairs. They appeared to be studying together.

"What is this?" Joel asked.

"ESL Class," Jorge explained.

"ESL?" Joel said. "Electric Sponge Licorice? Evil Smiling Lions?"

"Stop," Jorge said, laughing. "ESL is English as a Second Language."

Joel took a second look and realized that several of the people in the room were Latino or Asian.

"When people come here from other countries," Jorge said, "some of them speak English, but many do not. Can you imagine how hard it is to find a job or go to school here without knowing English?"

"Gosh," Joel said. "You couldn't read a menu or understand what they're saying on TV."

"In my family, we hope to become American citizens," Jorge said. "Learning English is the first thing we must do."

"Learning a new language is hard," Joel said. "Spanish class is killing me."

Jorge waved a hand toward the cafeteria. "These are the people who helped my family and me."

Joel peered into the room. The people at the tables seemed like ordinary folks. He recognized one woman who worked at his neighborhood library.

"These teachers do not get paid," Jorge told him. "Because they care, they give their time to help others learn. I think they are heroes."

Joel snapped a picture.

"Me, too," he said.

YOUR TURN

1. Besides teaching English, can you think of other ways to welcome strangers to your city or neighborhood?

_____

 PRAYER   God, what a great world it is when people help each other. I want to be a helper, too. Amen.

VOLUNTEERS NEEDED

Volunteers are needed in lots of places to do lots of things that help others. If you are going to look for ways to volunteer, it might be helpful to think about your own gifts and where they can best be used. Complete the survey below to get started thinking about what you might want to do and ask an adult to help you find a place that matches your interests and gifts.

If you had 2 hours to volunteer, what would you do?

1. a.____ work with children
   b.____ work with animals
   c.____ work with older adults

2. a.____ work indoors
   b.____ work outdoors
   c.____ work in a gym

3. a.____ talk to people
   b.____ work at a computer
   c.____ make phone calls

4. a.____ build something
   b.____ read something
   c.____ tell people how to do something

5. a.____ work with a friend
   b.____ work alone
   c.____ meet new people

■ A MISSION FROM GOD ■

God loves every living creature, not just people.

The LORD is good to all; he has compassion on all he has made.

– Psalm 145:9

GOING TO THE DOGS

"Hi, Mr. Bretz," Joel called, coasting his bicycle into the driveway of his Youth Group leader. "Looks like you're going for a drive."

"My wife and I make a long drive every Wednesday." Mr. Bretz leaned close to Joel and said, "We're on a mission from God."

Mrs. Bretz joined them beside the van. "Quit teasing," she said to her husband. She explained to Joel, "We help with an animal rescue mission."

"Lots of dogs get abandoned by their owners and end up in animal shelters," said Mr. Bretz. "Many of those dogs would make wonderful pets, and we help them find new homes."

"Once the dogs receive shots and the vet says they're healthy, there are people like us scattered around the country who drive them north," Mrs. Bretz said.

"Today a fellow from Kentucky is bringing us four dogs and we'll deliver them to Columbus," Mr. Bretz said. "Then we'll turn them over to another driver."

"Where do the dogs end up?" Joel asked.

"Canada," Mrs. Bretz said. "They do a wonderful job of finding homes for the dogs. Sometimes we get emails showing pictures of the dogs with their new families."

"This one looked so cute that I printed it," Mr. Bretz said.

Joel studied the picture of a floppy-eared dog being hugged by a little red-headed girl.

"We don't mind driving a hundred miles to find a loving home," Mrs. Bretz said, smiling at the picture.

"Can I use this picture in my project?" Joel asked.

"Sure," said Mr. Bretz. "Is your project about animals?"

"No," Joel said, climbing on his bike. "It's about heroes like you."

YOUR TURN

1. If you were going to look for a pet, would you go to a store or an animal rescue shelter? Why?

_____

 **PRAYER** God, help me to be kind to everyone I meet—even Your animals. Amen.

What Can i Do?

Some animals are heroes, too. They help people who have trouble seeing, hearing, or moving around.

If you like animals, call your local animal shelter and see what kinds of help they need. Your family may be able to volunteer by taking shelter dogs for walks.

Here's a recipe for dog treats that you can make and give to your friends who have dogs. This is a pretty easy recipe, but you might want to get adult help the first time you make it.

What To Do

1. First you'll need: 3 jars of meat-flavored baby food; ¼ cup dry milk powder; ¼ cup Cream of Wheat breakfast cereal; and ½ teaspoon garlic powder.

2. Dump everything together in a big bowl. Mix it well with a spoon.

3. Roll the goop into small balls and put it on a plate that is safe to go in the microwave. Squash the balls a little with a fork. You might want to spray the plate first with oil to keep the goodies from sticking.

4. Set the microwave on High and bake the treats for three or four minutes.

5. Let them cool before you try to handle them.

6. Keep them in the refrigerator and hope your dog doesn't figure out how to open the fridge door.

CARING FOR CREATION

God loves the world and wants us to take care of his creation.

When they had all had enough to eat, he said to his disciples,
"Gather the pieces that are left over. Let nothing be wasted."

– John 6:12

THE TRASH HUNTER

"Joel, pass me the meat loaf," Dad said, "and I'll pass something along to you in return."

"I really hope you're not planning to trade me the spinach for this delicious meat loaf," Joel said.

Dad handed Joel a newspaper clipping. Joel glanced at the headline: THE TRASH MAN.

"What's the article about?" Joel's mom asked.

"This guy named Berger drives around his town watching for good stuff in the garbage," Joel's dad explained. "When he sees something like a broken bicycle or an old vacuum sweeper, he takes it home and repairs it."

"That's great for the environment," Joel said. "We should all be recycling old things that still have some use left in them."

"That's right," his mother agreed. "Everything that fellow pulls from the trash would have ended up in a dump somewhere."

"He must have a garage full of toaster ovens and treadmills," Joel asked.

"He gives it away," Dad said. "Some of it goes to friends and neighbors, but he donates most of it to charity. The article says that every year Berger donates thousands of dollars worth of stuff to people in need."

"Wow!" Joel said. "He's helping the Earth and he's taking care of people, too."

"The reporter interviewed one of Berger's neighbors," Dad said. "The writer asked if people minded Berger grabbing their trash."

Joel scanned the article. "The neighbor says, 'No, we think Berger's a hero. One of these days, I hope he finds a cape in the trash. He deserves one.'"

"What do you think?" Dad asked. "Will you put Berger in your project?"

"Absolutely," Joel said. "Trash Man to the rescue!"

"I can't wait to see this project," Joel's mom said with a laugh.

YOUR TURN

1. Does it make any difference whether or not we recycle things?

_____

_____

PRAYER God, You made a world that can take care of us all, and we should be careful not to waste. Amen.

CARETAKERS OF OUR THINGS AND OURSELVES

It's good to go through your things to see what you are still using and what can be used by someone else. Sometimes there are things that should be thrown away so you have more room for the things you need. That's not only true for our possessions, but also for the way we think and act. Use the chart below to think about the usefulness of your things and actions.

	Things to keep	...to get rid of	...to share with others
Clothes			
Toys and games			
The way I treat people			
The way I use my time			

HEROES AT HOME

Loving each other begins at home.

Children, obey your parents in the Lord, for this is right.
– Ephesians 6:1

OVERTIME

"It's a good day to shoot some hoops," Joel said to his friend Rodrigo as they rode home on the school bus. "Can you come over today?"

"I have to fix supper for my little sister," Rodrigo said.

"Isn't your mom cooking?" Joel asked.

"Whenever her boss lets her work extra hours, she stays longer at her job," Rodrigo said. "They pay her well for the overtime."

"And you have to watch your sister," Joel said.

Rodrigo listed things on his fingers, counting them off one by one.

"I help Maria with her homework, cook dinner, wash the dishes, make sure she takes a bath, lay out her clothes for the next day, and get her in bed by nine o'clock."

"You must get tired," Joel said. "When do you do your homework?"

"After my sister is in bed," Rodrigo said. "If I can stay awake. My grades aren't so good."

"Why is your mom working so much?" Joel asked.

Rodrigo shrugged. "We need more money. Since Dad left, we can barely pay the rent on our apartment. Mom is riding the bus to work because we can't afford to repair our car."

Joel looked out the window, wondering what to say.

"I might get a job," Rodrigo said. "I could earn money raking leaves and doing chores for people on our street. Maybe then Mom wouldn't have to work so hard."

"I'm sorry things are so tough," Joel said.

"You don't have to feel sorry for me," Rodrigo said. "My mom is doing most of the work. She's the hero in my family."

"No," Joel said. "I think there's more than one hero in your family."

1. Do you have chores to do in your home? How do you feel about that?

_____

_____

PRAYER God, thanks for giving me a family. Show us how to take care of each other. Amen.

FAMILY SONGS

Think about how your family takes care of one another. Complete the songs by making up lyrics for the missing pieces. You can even sing these for your family at dinner!

Tune: Three Blind Mice

Helping _____

Helping _____

Makes me _____

Makes them _____

I won't be called a

_____ son

I'll do my work until it's done

And then I'll be ready for some fun,

(and) _____,

_____,

_____.

Tune: Twinkle, Twinkle Little Star

Picking up and _____

Makes my parents think I'm _____

If you need a _____

I will help you _____

Work goes faster if we share

Now you know I really care!

Tune: Row, row, row your boat

Help-ing ev' ry day,

_____

_____

_____.

SMOOTH OR CRUNCHY?

Helping the poor shows our love for them and for God.

If there is a poor man among your brothers... do not be
hardhearted or tightfisted toward your poor brother.
– Deuteronomy 15:7

HERO SANDWICHES

Granny smiled at Joel as he slid into the front seat with her.

"Hi, Sweetie," she said and kissed him on the cheek. "Thanks for going downtown with me today. You get to carry the bags."

"I'm glad to, Gran," Joel said.

They swapped jokes on the way. Finally, Gran parked the car and pointed to a large shoulder bag in the backseat. "Would you get that?" she asked.

"What's in this?" Joel asked, dragging it out.

"Just a few goodies," Gran said. "Never travel without food."

They strolled less than a block on the crowded sidewalk, before a ragged man with red eyes approached them.

"Could you spare a little change?" he said. "I haven't eaten since yesterday."

"I can do better than that," Gran said. She reached into the bag on Joel's shoulder and pulled out a sandwich wrapped in wax paper. She handed it to the man and said, "God bless."

On the next block another man came up to them. He squinted at Gran and said, "Hi, sandwich lady. Haven't seen you in a while."

Gran smiled at him. "Smooth or crunchy?"

"Crunchy, please." Over his shoulder he called into the alley behind him. "It's the sandwich lady."

A woman emerged, wearing three coats and pushing a shopping cart.

Gran said, "Hello, Millie! How are you, dear?" The woman held out her hand while staring at the ground. "Smooth for you, Millie. And here's an extra for later." Gran slipped a second sandwich in her shopping cart.

"This is your grandmother?" the man asked Joel. "She's a hero around here."

"Pish-posh," Gran said. "It doesn't take a hero to make peanut butter sandwiches."

YOUR TURN

1. Do you ever see homeless people begging for help? How does it make you feel?

_____

_____

PRAYER God, watch over the poor people today who have no place to sleep and nothing to eat. Amen.

WALK IN THEIR SHOES

What do you think it means to walk in someone else's shoes? Try to put yourself in the place of people who don't have a place to live and think about what their lives are like. Answer the questions below to help you get an idea of what it's like to walk in their shoes.

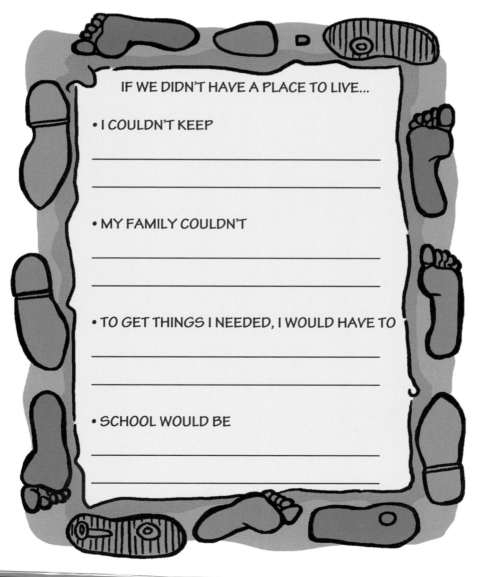

IF WE DIDN'T HAVE A PLACE TO LIVE...

• I COULDN'T KEEP

_____

_____

• MY FAMILY COULDN'T

_____

_____

• TO GET THINGS I NEEDED, I WOULD HAVE TO

_____

_____

• SCHOOL WOULD BE

_____

_____

■ THE BEST SUPER POWER ■

It pleases God when we give help to people who need it.

Look after orphans and widows in their distress...
– James 1:27

THE NEW DAUGHTER

Joel's mother said, "Would you set the table and then change into some clean clothes?"

"Are we having company?" Joel asked.

"The Eisners are coming for dinner," Mom said. "They're bringing their new daughter Rose."

Joel stopped with a bunch of forks in one hand and spoons in the other. "When did the Eisners get a new daughter?"

"The Eisners are Rose's foster parents," his mother explained.

"I don't know what that is," Joel said. He spread the silverware on the table and set a napkin at each place.

"Sometimes a child cannot stay with her natural parents," Mom said. She stirred vegetables in a skillet. "Maybe the parents die in an accident, and there are no relatives. Maybe the parents are in prison or drug treatment. A judge might decide that a home is unsafe for a child."

She sprinkled pepper in the pan and turned down the heat. "When things like that happen," she said, "children need a place to stay."

"Don't those kids go to orphanages or something?" Joel asked. He got glasses from the cabinet.

"They might," Mom said, "but most kids would rather be in a regular home with a real family."

"How long will Rose stay with the Eisners?" Joel asked.

"Maybe a week or two," Mom said. "Maybe years."

"Why are the Eisners doing this?" Joel said. "It sounds like a hassle. You know, getting a new kid, feeding them, buying clothes, and all that stuff."

His mother looked at him carefully and said, "They have taken in Rose because they are heroes, and their superpower is love."

"I guess that's the best power a hero can have," Joel said.

YOUR TURN

1. Would you be willing to let a new person join your family? Why?

_____

 **PRAYER**   God, thanks for loving kids so much and sending people to take care of us. Amen.

Families

Families come in lots of shapes and numbers. God made them all.
Connect the dots to build a house, then draw a picture of your family
inside it.

WARMING THE WORLD

Helping others shows our love for them and our love for God.

Suppose a brother or sister is without clothes.
If one of you says to him, "Go, I wish you well; keep warm
and well fed," but does nothing about his physical needs,
what good is it?

– James 2:15-16

COAT DRIVE

"Listen up everyone," the teacher said, "Tricia would like to talk to you about her class project."

Tricia stood before the class and shifted uneasily from foot to foot.

"I've been researching poverty in our city," she said, "I've learned that many people do not have warm clothes for the winter. Cold weather isn't far off. I decided I wanted to do more than read about the poor. I want to help."

She dragged a cardboard box to the front of the classroom. "So I'm starting a coat drive," she said. "If you have coats at home that you don't need, please bring them in."

"What happens then?" Joel asked.

"I found three shelters that will distribute the coats to needy people," she said. "They can use coats in all sizes, also hats, gloves, and scarves."

"Is it just our class doing this?" someone asked.

"Principal Simon says we can invite the entire school to take part," Tricia said, "but I can't do all that by myself." Her voice trailed off.

Mrs. O'Neill said, "Tricia is wondering if others would like to help. We will need volunteers to talk to other classes, put boxes around, and sort the coats as they come in. What do you think?"·

"My mom can get boxes at work," one boy offered.

"I can hand out fliers on my bus," a girl said.

"We can throw a party for the class that collects the most coats," another girl suggested.

"It looks like you're going to get plenty of help, Tricia," the teacher said.

Tricia nodded and smiled, her face blushing a bright red.

Joel decided she was the shyest hero he'd ever seen.

YOUR TURN

1. Does your church or school do things to help those who need help? Do you take part?

_____

PRAYER God, give me a heart to help people who need help. Amen.

COAT = LOVE

When someone doesn't have a coat, getting one means a whole lot of good things. Find words in the word search below that remind you of some of the things a coat might represent.

```
f l i f i w m u n s s w o p
c e a c a r i n g n a b p s
c h r o t r u d n s f k l f
w a r m t h s e b o e s h w
q p d p v t d r l e t a i x
c h p a s e b s c k y l t o
x r e s p e c t c h j r n q
z o u s x a w a r e n e s s
d u y i a c o n c e r n c h
d k t o c h l d h l d f o w
n s e n s i t i v i t y b k
x z m d h a i n o u r h g k
j o u e y y f g l e k s j r
```

WRAPPED IN LOVE

It pleases God when we show our love for people who are sad.

Blessed are those who mourn, for they will be comforted.

– Matthew 5:5

IN STITCHES

"Come in, Joel," Mrs. Gaiman said.

The elderly lady led Joel into her living room where a quilt was spread over the sofa. "I can't imagine why a young man would have any interest in an old lady's quilting."

He studied the quilt. It was a simple design, just blocks of different colors.

"When my mother died," Mrs. Gaiman said, "I missed her so much. I decided to make a quilt in her memory."

"How does this help you remember your mother?" Joel asked.

"I made it from her old clothes and belongings," Mrs. Gaiman explained. "Each block is cut from different fabric."

She pointed to a patch of faded blue.

"That's from Mother's apron," Mrs. Gaiman said. "The green square was taken from one of her favorite blouses. That square with the hula girl on it was a souvenir dish towel Mother bought during our trip to Hawaii."

Mrs. Gaiman ran her hand over the quilt and smiled.

"So many memories," she said. "When I wrap up in this, I feel like Mother is hugging me."

"Mom told me you make these quilts for other people, too," Joel said.

"When I hear that a friend has lost a loved one, I show them my quilt and ask if they'd like me to make one for them," Mrs. Gaiman said. "They bring me a pile of old clothes, and I take it from there. It's a little thing, but maybe it helps."

Joel snapped a picture of the quilt. "Thanks," he said. "This is just what I need for my project."

"A school report on quilts," Mrs. Gaiman said. "I never heard of such a curious thing."

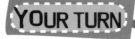

1. Is it good to remember people who have died? Why do you think that?

_____

_____

 God, I don't know what to say to people who are sad, but maybe a hug will help. Amen.

REMEMBERING

Make your own memory quilt for people and animals that you loved, but have died. Draw a picture or symbol in the squares to represent the people and then create designs in the squares that are left. Color your quilt. Is there someone you'd like to share your quilt and memories with?

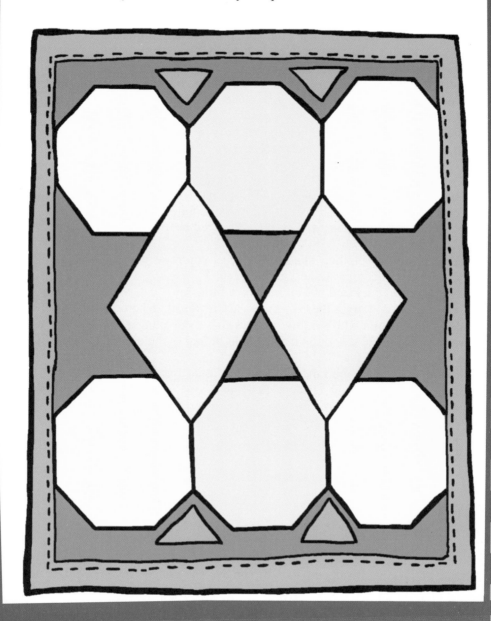

FUZZY, FURRY LOVE

Jesus loves children and wants us to watch over them.
*Jesus said, "Let the little children come to me,
and do not hinder them, for the kingdom of heaven
belongs to such as these."*
– Matthew 19:14

A BAG OF BEARS

"Joel, could you give me a hand?" Miss Giordano called across the church parking lot. She opened her car trunk and pointed to a large bag.

"My back isn't what it used to be," she said. "Would you please carry this inside for me?"

Joel lifted the bag from the trunk. It was bulky, but not too heavy. As they walked toward the church building, Joel asked, "What's in here?"

"Teddy bears," the woman said proudly. "I shop for them at garage sales and thrift shops. Only nice ones. Nothing raggedy or stained."

"Are we taking these to the church nursery?" Joel asked.

"They have plenty of toys already," she said. "We'll take these to the Ladies Aid room."

They entered the building and Joel set the bag in the room Miss Giordano led him to. She pulled out a pair of teddy bears. One was black and white like a panda, and the other was brown with a red heart sewed to its chest. She smiled at Joel.

"Thank you for helping," she said. "I'll bet you're wondering what an old lady is going to do with all these teddy bears."

"No, ma'am," Joel said. "Well, maybe a little."

"The Ladies Aid gives these to the local life squad. When the life squad comes to get a child who's injured or sick, it's frightening. If the emergency workers give the child a teddy bear to hold, it makes the child feel better. The bear takes away the fear."

"I have my camera with me," Joel said. "Could I get a picture of you?"

Miss Giordano held up a bear in each hand, and said, "I'm the pretty one in the middle."

YOUR TURN

1. Do children need more care than other people? Why do you think that?

_____

2. Why do you suppose Jesus enjoyed being with children?

_____

 **PRAYER** God, help me keep an eye on younger kids who might need my help. Amen.

KIDS NEED CARE

Look carefully at the pictures and find 5 things in picture #2 that are different from picture #1.

■ ORDINARY HEROES ■

God wants us to love each other.

Love your neighbor as yourself.
– Matthew 22:39

HEROES UNMASKED

My project is on heroes," Joel said, standing before the class. A picture of Superman appeared on the screen.

"Superman has great powers," Joel said, "but is that what makes a hero? What about ordinary people who do super things without super powers?"

He clicked the remote control and the picture on the screen changed to a man with thinning hair and round glasses.

"This is our own Principal, Mr. Simon," Joel said.

A boy in the back of the class called out, "Bring back Superman."

"Mr. Simon donates blood every two months," Joel said. "He has given over ten gallons of blood to save the lives of people in accidents and medical treatments. That makes him a hero to me."

Voices in the class murmured surprise and approval. The next picture showed a smiling woman in a sweatshirt.

"This is a woman in my church. She teaches adults to read so they can get better jobs."

"This man reads books aloud," Joel said, showing a man in a ball cap, "books that are recorded for blind people."

"This is my mom." Joel flashed a picture of his mother sitting at a piano. "She plays songs to entertain people in nursing homes."

The images flicked on the screen one after another, pictures of everyday people offering their time and energy to make the world better. None of the people looked special or amazing. None of them wore capes or helmets.

"All of these people are different," Joel said. "Here's what they have in common. They love others and they show their love. That makes them heroes. I want to be like these people. I hope you do, too, because there is always room for more heroes."

Joel got an "A" on his project.

1. When Jesus tells us to love our neighbor, what does he mean by neighbor?

_____

PRAYER God, there's a hero inside of everyone. Help me to let my hero out into the world. Amen.

LOTS OF KINDS OF HEROES

Anyone can be a hero. Some of your own friends or family members might be heroes. In the middle circle below, draw a picture of yourself. In the other circles write the name or draw the picture of people you know who are making the world a better place. You may add extra circles for even more heroes.

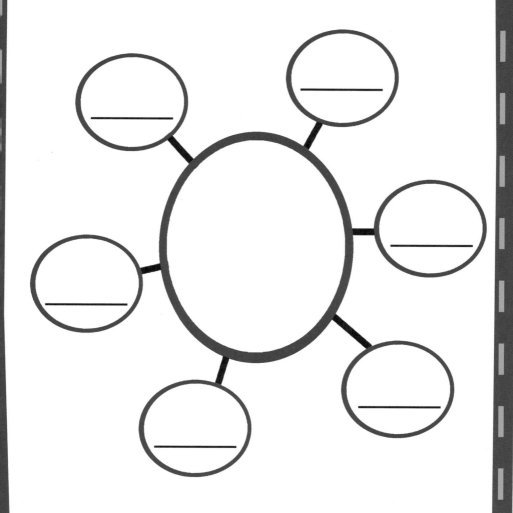

CHAPTER EIGHT

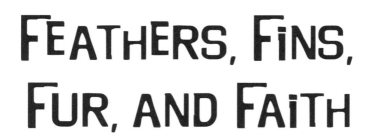

FEATHERS, FINS, FUR, AND FAITH

CARING FOR ONE ANOTHER
God wants us to help each other.
If you really keep the royal law found in Scripture,
"Love your neighbor as yourself," you are doing right.
– James 2:8

EATING BUGS

Mr. Maxwell led his Sunday school class into the bird house at the zoo where he worked.

"I love field trips," said Jason, "but I don't see how we're going to learn Christian stuff from birds."

"That's a good question, Jason," Mr. Maxwell said. "Let's start right here with this exhibit of huia birds."

The class stopped in front of a glass case that held two stuffed birds perched upon a log. Each bird was about eighteen inches long. They were covered in shiny black feathers with white tips.

"Those birds aren't even alive," Mike said.

"No, all the huia birds are dead now," said Mr. Maxwell sadly. "They were killed so their feathers could be used in hats."

"That's awful," Kylie said.

"Yes," agreed Mr. Maxwell. "We could have learned a lot from the huia birds."

"What could birds teach us?" asked Jason. "How to eat bugs?"

Everybody laughed, but Mr. Maxwell said, "That's right, Jason. Look at their beaks. The male has a wide beak shaped like a chisel. It was his job to chop away the tree bark that hid the bugs."

"The female has a skinny beak like tweezers," Kylie said.

"She poked into the bug holes and pulled them out," said Mr. Maxwell.

"So they worked together," Mike exclaimed. "They helped feed each other."

"Now who can tell me what the huia birds teach us?" Mr. Maxwell asked.

"That we should work together," Jason said.

"And take care of each other," Kylie added.

"Those were smart birds," Mr. Maxwell said.

"I wish everybody were that smart," Mike said.

YOUR TURN

1. What do you think the world would be like if we never helped each other?

_____

_____

 **PRAYER** Lord, I get a lot of help everyday from people who love me. I want to be helpful, too. Remind me to help others whenever I can. Amen.

WORKING TOGETHER

Mike and Jason want to build a dog house, but they must work together to get it done. Each boy has brought things for the job, but they need your help to put their tools and supplies together. Can you draw a line connecting the things that belong together in this job?

FORGETTING TO FLY

God gives us gifts so that we put them to use.

We have different gifts, according to the grace given us. If a man's gift is... serving, let him serve; if it is teaching, let him teach; if it is encouraging, let him encourage.
– Romans 12:6-8

LAZY BONES

"It's another dead bird," Jason said.

Inside the display case was a bird skeleton standing about three feet tall. The skeleton had long legs and a big beak.

"That was a dodo," Mr. Maxwell said.

The Sunday school class gathered around their teacher as he spoke. He had promised to teach them Christian lessons during their zoo field trip.

"The dodos are all gone now," Mr. Maxwell explained. "Long ago they were smaller and were able to fly, but they landed on an island in the Indian Ocean and settled down there. On the island, there were no wolves or cats, nothing to hurt them."

"That sounds great for the dodos," Kylie said. "Those lucky birds."

"Life was so easy for the dodos," Mr. Maxwell said, "that they got lazy. Food was easy to find and nothing chased them, so they stopped flying."

"I'll bet their wings got weak," Mike said. "When I got the cast off my leg, the muscles were flabby."

"Yes," the teacher agreed. "As the birds had babies and grandbabies and great grandbabies, their wings got smaller and smaller until the dodos could no longer fly."

"That's so sad," Kylie said.

"It's a waste of wings," Jason added.

"It's a little of both," Mr. Maxwell told them. "And there's a lesson here for us. When God gives us gifts, we're supposed to use them. If you're a singer who doesn't sing, or a reader who doesn't read, your gifts are going to waste. It's like having wings without flying. Having gifts we don't use is like not having gifts at all. Any questions?"

"Yeah," Jason said, "are there any live birds in this place?"

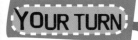

1. What are some of the gifts that God gave you? How can you make sure they don't go to waste?

_____

God, thanks for giving me things I'm good at. I want to use my gifts so everyone will see how good You've been to me. Amen.

PUTTING OUR GIFTS TO WORK

God gives different gifts to each of us, and God wants us to use those gifts. Do you wonder why God makes sure that each of His children has gifts to use? 1 Corinthians 3:9 tells us the answer.

The message is below. Ooops! Someone left out the spaces between words and removed all the A's, E's, and O's. Can you figure it out anyway? (Hint: There are six words in the sentence.)

FRWRGD'SFLLWWRKRS.

_____ .

RISKY LOVE

Jesus loved us so much that he died for us.
For Christ died for sins once for all, the righteous for the unrighteous, to bring you to God.
– I Peter 3:18

A BRAVE BIRD

"What kind of bird is this?" Jason asked.

In a glass cage was a brown bird with a white belly that had two black stripes. The inside of the cage looked like a field. A nest sat on the floor, among patches of grass.

Mr. Maxwell said, "This is the killdeer. It's one of my favorite birds."

"Does it make a pretty song?" Kylie asked.

"Not really," Mr. Maxwell said. "It's not a songbird."

"Then why do you like it?" Kylie asked her teacher.

"Notice that the killdeer builds its nest on the ground," Mr. Maxwell explained. "If a cat or a fox finds the nest, what happens to the babies?"

"They get eaten," Mike said.

"But hungry animals don't usually find the nest, because the momma killdeer is an actress," Mr. Maxwell said with a chuckle. "She fakes a broken wing and drags herself on the ground away from the nest. The hungry fox follows, thinking she's an each catch, but when they get far away from the nest, the mother flies away and leaves the disappointed fox behind."

"You go, killdeer," Jason said.

"It's dangerous for the killdeer," Mr. Maxwell said. "Sometimes the fox or the snake is too fast, but the mother bird is willing to die for her babies."

"Just like Jesus," Kylie said.

Mr. Maxwell smiled. "Tell us more, Kylie," he said.

"Jesus died on the cross so that we could escape from our sins," Kylie said. "He died to save us."

"That's right, Kylie," Mr. Maxwell agreed. "Jesus died for you and me."

"Wow!" Mike said. "There really is a lot we can learn from the birds."

YOUR TURN

1. It would take a lot of love to die for somebody. How do you feel knowing that Jesus loves you that much?

_____

_____

PRAYER   God, thank You for sending Jesus to die for me. I can hardly believe how big Your love is! Amen.

On The Cross

Do you believe Jesus died to save you from sin? If you believe that, write your name on the cross below.

Invite someone else who also believes in Jesus to add their name to the cross, too—maybe someone in your family.

Do you think you can fill the cross with signatures from Christians you know? How many names do you think you can squeeze onto this cross? Where would be a good place to collect signatures? Church? Sunday school? Your neighborhood? The dinner table?

■ OVERSHADOWED ■

God always watches over us to keep us safe.

He who dwells in the shelter of the Most High
will rest in the shadow of the Almighty.
– Psalm 91:1

SAFE IN THE SHADE

"Here's a bird that fascinates me," Mr. Maxwell said.

The Sunday school class gathered around the cage and looked at a bird about a foot long. It had long legs and its feathers were splashed with blotches of black and white.

"The blacksmith plover lives in Africa," Mike said, reading from the sign on the cage. "It scoops a hole in the ground and lays eggs there."

"That's where it gets interesting," Mr. Maxwell said. "At night when the air becomes cool, the mother and father birds take turns sitting on the eggs and keeping them warm."

"Do they leave the eggs during the day?" Kylie asked.

"In the daytime it gets extremely hot in Africa," Mr. Maxwell said. "The eggs may get too hot."

"Boiled plover eggs," Mike said.

"In the hottest part of the day," Mr. Maxwell said, "the plover mom or dad stands beside the nest and spreads its wings to make shade for the eggs."

"That sounds hard," Mike said, "standing there for hours in the heat."

The kids thought about how it feels to be in the sun on a hot day with nowhere to hide from the heat.

"The people who wrote the Bible knew about living in the desert," Mr. Maxwell said. "They understood how powerful the desert sun can be. Sometimes they thought of God as a shade from the noon heat."

"I don't get it," Mike said.

"In the desert," Jason said, "shade protects and comforts people. Isn't that what God does for us?"

"You've got it figured out," Mr. Maxwell said.

"I guess you could say that God takes the heat for us," Jason said, grinning.

1. Do you think there have been times when God protected you from danger and you never knew it?

___

PRAYER God, I like sunny days, but I always want to be in Your shadow so You can take care of me. Amen.

GOD THE PROTECTOR

The Bible talks about God's protection in different ways. Look up each of these passages to find new ways of picturing God's protective love. From the Bible verses, choose some ideas that help you think about God's protection and draw those on the picture below. Draw protection between the boy and each of the threats. What kinds of protection can shield against these threats?

Deuteronomy 33:29

Exodus 15:6

Psalm 62:2

Proverbs 18:10

FILLED UP

Looking for good things in life helps us find them.

The mind controlled by the Spirit is life and peace.
– Romans 8:6

HONEY OR ROAD KILL?

"Oooooh, I love hummingbirds," Kylie said.

Tiny, bright-colored birds flitted around, their wings a rapid blur in the cage.

"My grandparents have a hummingbird feeder, and lots of them come to eat sugar water," Mike said. "One landed on my hand once."

"In the wild, hummingbirds drink the nectar from flowers," Mr. Maxwell said.

"That means they live on honey, right?" asked Mike.

"Exactly right," Mr. Maxwell agreed. "Not all birds have such a delicate diet. Remember the vulture we saw a few minutes ago? Do you know what they eat?"

"Dead things," Mike said.

Mr. Maxwell nodded.

"You'll find both vultures and hummingbirds living in the desert," he said. "The hummingbirds spend their time searching for flowers and filling themselves with sweetness. The vultures soar all day looking for dead animals and they stuff themselves with rotting flesh and decay."

"Yuck," said Kylie.

Mike and Jason grinned at each other. In unison they said, "Is there a lesson there for us, Mr. Maxwell?"

"You're getting the hang of this," he said. "Can you guess what the lesson is?"

"Never have lunch with a vulture," Jason said.

"I had a different lesson in mind," Mr. Maxwell told them. "There are two ways to live. We can be vultures who fill our lives with rotten, unhealthy things like gossip, envy, anger, and bad feelings. Or we can be hummingbirds who fill ourselves with good things like prayer, friendship, generosity, and love. The choice is up to you."

"I'd rather have a honey sandwich than a dead skunk burger," Kylie said.

"Whatever you look for in life," Mr. Maxwell said, "that's what you'll find—just like the vulture and the hummingbird."

YOUR TURN

1. Think about your favorite music, TV, and books. Are you more like a vulture or a hummingbird?

PRAYER   God, my day is going to have all kinds of stuff in it. Help me look for the good things. Amen.

MAKING YOUR OWN HONEY SANDWICH

Wouldn't you rather have a honey sandwich than a rotten skunk burger? Here's the way to make sure your life is filled with thoughts and deeds that will lift you up instead of concerns that will drag you down. This advice comes from chapter 4 of Paul's letter to the Philippians.

To break the code, move each letter back one space in the alphabet. So F becomes E, and X becomes W.

XIBUFWFS   JT   USVF,

XIBUFWFS   JT   OPCMF,

XIBUFWFS   JT   SJHIU,

XIBUFWFS   JT   QVSF,

XIBUFWFS   JT   MPWFMZ,

XIBUFWFS   JT   BENJSBCMF,

UIJOL BCPVU TVDI UIJOHT.

JESUS OUR LEADER
Being a Christian means following Jesus.

"Follow me," he told him, and Matthew got up and followed him.
– Matthew 9:9

FOLLOW THOSE TAIL FEATHERS!

As Mr. Maxwell's Sunday school class studied the hummingbirds, a zoo worker approached.

"The ducklings are on their way to the lake for lunch," he told them.

The class hurried outside in time to see a mother duck waddling along the sidewalk followed by seven fluffy ducklings in a straight line.

"I'll bet your school teachers wish you would line up like that," Mr. Maxwell joked.

"Wow!" Jason said. "Did the zoo keeper train those little ducks to do that?"

"God taught them to do that," Mr. Maxwell said with a smile. "When ducklings hatch, they follow the first thing they see moving."

"So if the first thing they saw was a cat," Mike asked, "the baby ducks would follow it?"

"That wouldn't turn out well," Kylie said.

"Yeah, the mother duck leads them to food and water," said Jason, "but a cat leads the baby ducks right into his own mouth."

"We have to be careful who we follow," Mr. Maxwell agreed. "If we follow a bad leader, we'll get in trouble."

"How can we tell a good leader from a bad one?" Kylie asked.

"A good leader cares about his followers and takes care of them," Mr. Maxwell said. "A good leader wouldn't ask you to do something bad or to keep secrets from parents and friends."

"Jesus is the best leader," Mike said.

"He's led me for many years," Mr. Maxwell said. "He's never failed me."

"How do we know what Jesus wants us to do?" Kylie asked.

"Study the Bible, pray, and spend time with other Christians," Mr. Maxwell said. "If you do those things, you'll stay lined up behind your leader."

YOUR TURN

1. Can you think of people who would lead you into trouble if you followed them?

_____

_____

PRAYER

Jesus, I want to follow You today. I know You'll always lead me to the right place. Amen.

FOLLOWING JESUS

Following Jesus might lead to surprises sometimes, but we can be pretty sure there are some places where Jesus would never lead us.

See if you can follow Jesus through the maze below. Watch out for the dead-ends!

HIGH AND LOW

Nothing is hidden from God's eyes.
*The eyes of the LORD are on the righteous
and his ears are attentive to their cry.*
– Psalm 34:15

HAWK EYES

The red tailed hawk perched on a tree limb in a large outdoor enclosure near the birdhouse at the zoo. His tail feathers were the color of rusty iron. The bird spread broad brown wings and turned to fix cold eyes upon the kids on the Sunday school field trip.

"He's looking us over," Jason said.

"He can see us better than we can see him," Kylie said. "Hawks have amazing eyesight."

"But his eyes are tiny," Mike said.

"Kylie's right," Mr. Maxwell said. "If that bird could read, he could sit on top of a seven story building and read a newspaper on the street below."

"I couldn't do that even with binoculars," Mike said. He pushed his glasses up on the bridge of his nose.

"He wouldn't mind sitting in the back row at the movies," Sarah said.

"A hawk can sit on top of a light post and see a mouse running through a field a mile away," Mr. Maxwell continued.

"I can spot a burger restaurant a mile away," Jason joked, and the other kids laughed.

"But God has even better eyes than the hawk," Mr. Maxwell. "The Lord keeps an eye on you and me no matter where we go."

"Everybody at once?" Mike asked.

"Yes," Mr. Maxwell told him. "Right now God sees cave explorers, astronauts in orbit, and divers at the bottom of the sea. He sees where we've been and where we're going."

"God sees things that haven't happened yet?" Kylie asked.

"Oh, yes," the teacher said.

"I wish I could look into the future," Jason said, "to see what I'm having for dinner tonight."

YOUR TURN

1. If God can see into your heart and your thoughts, does that mean God always understands how you feel? Does anyone else know you as well as God does?

 **PRAYER**   God, You can see when I need help even before I do. I'm so glad You always keep an eye on me. Thanks.

KEEPING WATCH

God always keeps an eye on us. We may feel like we're in trouble, but God is still watching over us. Here are some people God watched over during scary and dangerous times. Can you name each person? You can look it up in your Bible if you don't recognize everyone.

Genesis 8:1

Daniel 6:16

1 Kings 17:44-45

Judges 14:5-6

Acts 16:22-26

■ COUNTING HAIRS ■

God can help with anything that comes, no matter how big or small.

And even the very hairs of your head are all numbered.
– Matthew 10:30

FURRY FEET

"Let's visit the polar bear cage," Mr. Maxwell said.

The teacher led his Sunday school class across the zoo to a pool where two white bears swam and splashed each other.

"They can swim!" shouted Mike.

"Polar bears are excellent swimmers," Mr. Maxwell said. "A healthy polar bear with plenty of fat can swim a hundred miles without stopping."

"Fat?" Mike asked.

"The fat keeps the bear warm and helps him float," the teacher explained. "But swimming isn't the most unusual thing about polar bears. Take a good look at their feet."

"They have big claws," Jason said.

"What else do you see on their feet?" Mr. Maxwell asked.

"Hair!" Mike said.

"Good job, Mike," Mr. Maxwell said. "The polar bear actually has hair on the bottom of its feet."

"God gave the polar bear hairy soles so that his feet won't get cold while he walks on snow and ice?" Jason guessed.

"I think so," Mr. Maxwell said. "God doesn't miss even the smallest thing."

"A hair is pretty small," Mike said.

"Yes, it is, but God has counted every hair on your head, Mike," Mr. Maxwell said. "God sees if a single hair falls off on your pillow."

"I hear a lesson coming," Kylie said with a laugh.

"If God takes care of polar bears, he will also take care of you," Mr. Maxwell said. "And if God notices every hair on your head, do you think he's going to overlook anything you need?"

YOUR TURN

1. Do you think worrying helps make things turn out better? Why do people spend so much time worrying?

_____

PRAYER God, I don't know why I worry. Nothing is too big or too little for You to handle, so I'm turning all my problems over to You. Okay?

FANTASTIC FEET

God promises not to let your foot slip! To keep that promise, God has invented some amazing feet. See if you can match the statements below with the right animal. Draw a line to connect each sentence with the animal that it describes.

ANIMALS

STATEMENTS

I have claws that give me traction for fast running.

I have feet that can taste flowers.

I have feet that let me walk on the ceiling.

I have locking feet so I can sleep on a branch without falling.

My flat feet help me swim.

I have hundreds of feet for creeping everywhere.

I use my clawed feet to dig under the earth.

CAN YOU HEAR ME NOW?

God hears every prayer we pray.

I call on you, O God, for you will answer me;
give ear to me and hear my prayer.

– Psalm 17:6

BAT SIGNALS

Mr. Maxwell's Sunday school class entered the dimly lit nocturnal house at the zoo.

"These animals are active in the night," Jason said. "I've been here before. Let me show you the bats."

They followed Jason to several glass cases that contained bats. In one exhibit were giant fruit bats. When they spread their wings, it measured almost five feet from tip to tip.

"I wouldn't want to bump into one of those," Mike said.

Another case held small brown bats, hanging upside down from branches.

"These are the bats you see flying over your back yard on a summer night," said Mr. Maxwell.

"They eat mosquitoes," Jason said.

"And they find them with their ears," Mike added. "They use radar."

"That's right," Mr. Maxwell said. "Bats don't see very well, but they have amazing hearing."

"Do they lay eggs?" Kylie asked.

"No, they have live babies," their teacher explained. "The babies hang on a cave wall while the mothers hunt for food. In a large colony of bats there may be thousands of babies hanging on the stone. When a mother returns, all the babies screech, hoping to be fed."

"Wow," Kylie said. "How does the mother find her baby?"

"By listening," Mr. Maxwell told her. "Among thousands of screams, the mother can recognize the cry of her own child and fly straight to that baby. In this way, bat mothers are a little like God. With all the noise in the world, God hears the softest prayer. There must be millions of people talking to God right now, but God hears each one and recognizes the voice of each of his children."

YOUR TURN

1. Do you ever wonder if God pays attention to your prayers?

_____

 God, even the people in my family don't always pay attention to me, but You always listen. Thanks for having time for me. Amen.

NO BUSY SIGNAL

Do you ever phone someone and get a busy signal? Have you ever sent an email and it got lost in space? That doesn't happen with prayer! God is never too busy or distracted to get our messages.

In the third chapter of his first letter, Peter promises that God will pay attention to his children. If you want to read that promise, remove every B and J and M and Q and X and Z from the message below. Then add a few spaces, and you'll have it solved.

MTBHQEJEYZXESBOFTJHMQELZOXRDBWQA

JTZCMHOXVEBQRJTXHZMOSEWHXOQJDBORIX

ZGMHTAJNDHMBIQSJZEAXMRSAQBREMJOZP

XBJMQENTOTBHEQBJIRPXRZABJZQYXMERS.

GETTING STRONG
God brings good out of bad.

*And we know that in all things God works for the good of those
who love him, who have been called according to his purpose.*
                                                        – Romans 8:28

SPREADING WINGS

The field trip had entered the insect house. In a glass case, a cocoon hung
from a twig. One end of the cocoon was torn open and a bug was squeezing
itself through the tear.

"It's a cecropia moth," Mr. Maxwell explained. "We're lucky to be here at
the right time to watch the moth come out of its cocoon."

The moth squeezed its head free and struggled to press further into the light.

"So this used to be a caterpillar," Jason said. "Then it made a cocoon for
itself where it turned into a moth."

"We're watching a crawler turning into a flyer," said Mr. Maxwell.

The moth pushed against the cocoon, but seemed stuck.

"The poor thing is having a hard time," Kylie said.

"Yeah," Mike said. "I wish I could tear that cocoon open for him. Then he
wouldn't have to work so hard."

"It's a good thing you can't help him," their teacher said. "You'd make
things much worse."

"What do you mean?" Mike asked. "I'd be careful. I wouldn't hurt him."

"Mike," said Mr. Maxwell, "you mean well, but the moth needs this
struggle. His hard work is forcing blood into his wings so they will be strong.
If you helped him out of the cocoon, his wings would be shriveled. He'd
never fly."

The moth stopped moving for a moment, then wriggled slowly free from
the cocoon. His brightly patterned wings slowly spread out.

"Yay, moth!" Mike said. "Now you can fly."

"Yes," agreed Mr. Maxwell. "God used its hard work to make a good thing
happen. He does that for moths and for people, too."

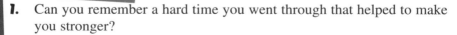

YOUR TURN

1. Can you remember a hard time you went through that helped to make
you stronger?

_____

_____

PRAYER God, I don't always know Your plan, but I believe You
are using the hard things to make me a stronger and better
person. Let's work together always. Amen.

BAD INTO GOOD

The book of Genesis tells the story of Joseph. Many bad things happened to him, but God used it for good. You can help tell Joseph's story by filling in the blanks.

Joseph's brothers hated him and threw him into a
__ __ __ (rhymes with spit). Then they sold him as a
__ __ __ __ __ (rhymes with crave). Poor Joseph was
carried to Egypt. A woman lied about him and got Joseph
in __ __ __ __ __ __ __ __ (rhymes with bubble). He
ended up in __ __ __ __ (rhymes with rail). A government
official promised to help Joseph, but he __ __ __ __ __
__ (rhymes with robot). Finally God raised Joseph to take
an important __ __ __ __ __ __ __ __ (rhymes with
physician) in Egypt. Joseph was able to save the country
from __ __ __ __ __ __ (rhymes with younger). He even
saved his own family from __ __ __ __ __ (rhymes with
flying). When Joseph's brothers said they were
__ __ __ __ __ (rhymes with starry), Joseph told them,
"You meant __ __ __ __ (rhymes with weevil) for me, but
God used it for __ __ __ __ (rhymes with hood).

GOD NEVER NAPS

God is always on the job.
He who watches over you will not slumber.
– Psalm 121:3

SLEEPING WITH ONE EYE OPEN

Mr. Maxwell's class cheered as the dolphin danced across the surface of the pool, balanced on its tail. The field trip had moved to the aquarium section of the zoo.

"Our zoo has a great collection of water animals," Mr. Maxwell said when the dolphin act ended.

"What a smart fish," Mike said.

"A dolphin isn't a fish," Jason said. "They breathe air like us."

"Sure," said Kylie. "They come to the surface to breathe."

"If a dolphin is wounded," said Mr. Maxwell, "the other dolphins will take turns lifting it to the surface."

"That's so cool," Mike said.

"How do dolphins sleep without drowning?" Jason asked.

"Dolphins never go completely to sleep," Mr. Maxwell explained. "A dolphin closes one eye at a time and lets half of his brain go to sleep. The other half of the dolphin's brain keeps the animal swimming and breathing."

"Do the eyes take turns?" Mike asked.

"Yes, after a while the eyes trade off," said their teacher, "and one half of the brain wakes up while the other naps."

"So dolphins are always awake," Kylie said.

"That's right," Mr. Maxwell agreed, "just like God. Our Lord never dozes off. God is always wide awake. Every second of every day, God is running the universe and protecting us."

"That's good," Mike said. "I need a little help from God right now, and I'm glad He's not napping."

"What kind of help?" Mr. Maxwell asked, sounding concerned.

"Remember that huge soda I drank?" Mike said.

"Yes," Mr. Maxwell said. "Are you feeling ill?"

"No, I feel fine," Mike said, "but I hope God helps me find a restroom soon."

YOUR TURN

1. When you go to sleep at night, how does it make you feel to know that God is wide awake?

_____

PRAYER God, I'll get in bed tonight without any worries or fears because I know You never go to sleep. Thanks for being on the job! Amen.

EYE EXAM

Have you ever had to read those crazy vision charts in the eye doctor's office? How did you do? Here's one that won't give you any trouble. Just go through the chart, beginning at the top line, working your way left to right, and write down all the letters that are red. Next, start over and write the letters that are yellow. Then write the letters that are blue. When you get through, you'll find out how God can watch over you all the time.

Fill in the letters here:

___ ___ ___ ___ ___ ___ ___ ___

___ ___ ___ ___ ___

N G S
E O L V E
E E P D R S

■ FLASHLIGHT CHRISTIANS ■

Jesus wants us to share His light with the world.

Let your light shine before men, that they may see your good deeds and praise your Father in heaven.
– Matthew 5:16

WHERE THE SUN NEVER SHINES

"This is the best field trip ever!" Jason said as the class entered the zoo aquarium. "Are there other sea creatures we can learn from?"

"How about the lanternfish?" Mr. Maxwell asked. "Lanternfish live in very deep ocean water where it's always as dark as midnight."

Mr. Maxwell led the group to a poster. He pointed to a picture of a short, stubby fish with bulging eyes. A wormy length of flesh poked from its forehead like a saggy antenna.

"That's a lanternfish? If I looked like that, I'd live in the dark for sure," Mike said.

"Why is it called a lanternfish?" Kylie asked.

"Maybe it carries a waterproof flashlight," Mike suggested.

"Almost right," Mr. Maxwell said. "The lanternfish provides its own flashlight. See that thing that looks like a droopy antenna sticking out of its head? That antenna glows in the dark."

"I wish I could shine in the dark," Jason said. "That would be so cool."

"You can shine," the teacher said. "All of us can. Jesus said that Christians are the light of the world. It is our job to light up the world by showing God's love."

"We can do that by doing good deeds," Jason said.

Mr. Maxwell said, "You shine for God every time the youth group visits a nursing home and spends time with lonely people. You are shining when you help little kids with homework in the after-school program at church. You shine when you forgive someone or welcome a new kid at school."

"Alright!" Jason said, pumping his fist in the air. "I can be a lanternfish for Jesus!"

YOUR TURN

1. What could you do today to "light up" your home and family?

_____

PRAYER

God, when people look at the way I live, I want them to think of You! Amen.

SHINE YOUR LIGHT

Jesus wants us to shine with God's love and goodness, so that we will be a blessing to others. Maybe these stories will help you figure out how to shine in your life. Each story is unfinished. You need to add endings that will show the characters how to shine.

■ Cameron lives next door to an older woman who uses a cane to walk. Last week she fell on the ice when trying to take her garbage can to the street. How can Cameron shine?

My Ending: _____

■ Elijah rides the bus with a boy who is failing in science class. Elijah gets all "A"s in science. How can Elijah shine?

My Ending: _____

■ Frank walks through the park each day on his way to school. It bothers him that there is so much garbage and litter on the playground. How can Frank shine?

My Ending: _____

■ Colt's little brother wants to hang out with Colt and his friends all the time. Sometimes it really bugs Colt that his brother is always around. How can Colt shine?

My Ending: _____

WASHED UP

Through the death and resurrection of Jesus, God washes away our sins.

He saved us through the washing of rebirth and renewal by the Holy Spirit.
– Titus 3:5

THE CLEANING STATION

"I can think of another fish that might teach us a lesson," Mr. Maxwell said. With a grin, he added, "I just happen to have a science video about the cleaner wrasse fish."

The Sunday school class was in the church van, heading home after their zoo field trip. When the van stopped at a red light, Mr. Maxwell slid a DVD into the van's movie player. The small screen showed a thin fish with blue and black stripes running along its sides.

"Fish sometimes get parasites and pests that dig into their scales and gills. These pests can make a fish sick or even kill it," Mr. Maxwell explained.

"Without hands, it must be hard for fish to clean themselves," Kylie said.

"The cleaner wrasses set up cleaning stations," Mr. Maxwell said. "Other fish come to get rid of their parasites and pests."

"How does that work?" Jason asked.

"Several cleaner wrasses pick a spot and hang out there. Other fish come for cleaning. The wrasses pluck dirt and parasites from their gills and scales."

On the movie screen, an eel opened its mouth wide while a wrasse cleaned its teeth and gums.

"Fish that might normally eat the others call a truce so everyone can get cleaned," the teacher said.

"It sounds like the church," Jason said. "We come with our sins, and Jesus cleans us up. All different kinds of people come to church, but we all need cleaning."

"I agree, Jason," said Mr. Maxwell. "I think the church is a lot like a cleaning station."

"I can't wait to tell Pastor Chris that there is something fishy about our church," Jason said.

YOUR TURN

1. Do you ever talk to God about the mistakes you've made and the things you've done wrong?

_____

PRAYER God, thanks for sending Jesus to wash me clean and take away my sins. Amen.

ALL CLEANED UP

How wonderful that God forgives our sins and washes us clean with the love of Jesus! After we have been forgiven, do you know how we look in God's eyes? Fill in each bubble below that contains any of these letters: F-O-R-G-I-V-E. When you've finished, the filled in bubbles will reveal how you look to God.

MADE FOR EACH OTHER

In Jesus, we all belong to one family of God.
Let us not give up meeting together, as some are in the habit of doing, but let us encourage one another.
– Hebrews 10:25

ALL IN THE FAMILY

"We're almost back to church," said Mr. Maxwell as he steered the van. "I hope you've enjoyed our zoo field trip."

"It's been great!" Jason said. "I've learned so much from the animals."

"Me too," said Mike, waking from a nap.

"We have time for a few quick animal riddles," Mr. Maxwell said. "Most animals live in groups so they can be safer. Does anyone know the name used for a group of dolphins?"

"A pod," Kylie said.

"Good," said Mr. Maxwell. "What about a group of crows?"

"I know!" said Jason. "A murder of crows."

"I'll have to make this tougher," said Mr. Maxwell. "How about a group of lions?"

"A pride," Mike said. "We are so hot!"

Mr. Maxwell smiled. "How about a group of turtles?"

The kids looked at each other shrugged.

"A bale of turtles," Mr. Maxwell said.

"Tell us more," Jason said.

"Let's see," Mr. Maxwell pondered. "A smack of jellyfish, a knot of toads, and a shiver of sharks."

"One more," Jason pleaded as the church came in sight.

"A passel of possums," Mr. Maxwell said.

There was more laughter.

"Okay, here's the last question," Mr. Maxwell said as he turned the van into the church parking lot. "What is the name for a bunch of Christians?"

"Church!" Mike and Kylie shouted in unison.

"That's right," Mr. Maxwell agreed. "Jesus doesn't want his followers to go it alone, so he gives us to each other and puts us together."

"The Jesus club," Jason said.

"Better than that," Mr. Maxwell said. "We're the Jesus family."

YOUR TURN

1. Do you like going to church? What are your favorite parts of church?

_____

PRAYER   God, help me be a good member of Your family, the church. Amen.

ANIMAL FAMILIES

Some animals are loners, but most animals hang together in families and groups, just like Christians do. Here are some of the funny names given to different animal groups. First you have to unscramble the family names. Then you have to match the animal with its family. You might need some family help on this one!

PLAE of leopards

_____

LEPRKIC of porcupines

_____

RAHCS of rhinos

_____

TRFA of sea otters

_____

RTWEO of giraffes

_____

LEAGGG of geese

_____

YOCONL of bats

_____

LOBAT of hippos

_____

KLCECA of hyenas

_____

ARHMC of
hummingbirds

_____

CHAPTER NINE

WHEN THINGS GO WRONG

COUNTING BLESSINGS

Even when things go wrong, we can still find reasons to be thankful.

Give thanks in all circumstances...
– I Thessalonians 5:18

THE CRUMMIEST SUMMER

Jeremy and his older brother Reese were watching television. Jeremy lay on the sofa. His left ankle, wrapped in a heavy cast, was propped on a pillow.

"What a rotten time to break my ankle," Jeremy grumbled.

Reese stared at the television.

"No swimming, no soccer, no fun," Jeremy said. "This is going to be the worst summer ever."

"Your complaining is driving me crazy," Reese said.

"I've got plenty to complain about," Jeremy said angrily.

"You've got even more to be thankful for," Reese said. "One, when you fell off your skate board, you broke your ankle instead of your neck. Two, it's a clean break and will heal up fine."

"Three," said Jeremy, "my brother is a pain in the neck."

"I'm not finished," Reese said. "Three, you live in a country with great doctors. Four, your family can afford to take you to the doctor. Five, you'll be walking again in a few weeks, but some people can never walk. Six, you've got books to read, movies to watch, and food to eat."

"You're a big help," Jeremy said. "Do you think this cast is fun?"

In a gentle voice Reese said, "I'm sorry you got hurt. But if you have a lousy, awful summer, don't blame your ankle. Blame your attitude. You can complain or you can practice being thankful. Which do you think will make a better summer?"

Jeremy frowned.

"Maybe a root beer float would help you think things over," Reese said.

"Maybe it would," said Jeremy.

"Okay, I'll make you one," Reese said, "and you can add me to the list of things you're thankful for."

YOUR TURN

1. When you complain about things, how does it make you feel? What about when you think about good things?

_____

 God, there are so many good things in my life that I can't count them all. Thank You for all Your blessings. Amen.

THANKS GIVER OR GRUMPY LIVER?

It's easy to complain about the things that have gone wrong for us, but sometimes we aren't very good at remembering the things that are going right. The more we practice giving thanks to God, the more good things we find to be glad about.

In the picture below, unscramble the mixed up words to find some things that Jeremy is thankful for. As a clue, the first letter of each word is capitalized. In the empty spaces, you can write or draw good things from your own life.

OVERCOMERS

With God's help, we can overcome obstacles and problems.
No, in all these things we are more than conquerors through him who loved us.
– Romans 8:37

ROLLING

Jeremy's brother punched the television remote and changed channels. A sporting event replaced a cartoon.

"Hey!" Jeremy said. "Who made you boss of the television?"

"You've got to see this," Reese said.

Jeremy shifted his leg on the pillow, adjusting the cast on his broken ankle.

"If I weren't stuck in this recliner..." Jeremy said.

"Yeah, I'm shaking with fear," Reese said. He nodded toward the television. "Check this out"

On the screen two teams raced and circled on a basketball court. The action was fast, the passing smooth, and the shooting excellent. It was like many games Jeremy had seen, except that every player was in a wheelchair. The players wheeled around the court at dizzying speeds, racing up and down the floor while dribbling and passing.

"These guys are great," Jeremy said.

"Wheelchair athletes," Reese said. "How cool is this?"

The players rolled across the floor, interweaving but never crashing.

"A couple of these guys are marathoners," Reese said.

"Twenty-six miles at top speed in a wheelchair?" Jeremy asked. "Wow. They must have arm muscles like Superman."

"Believe it, little brother," Reese said. "You won't find better athletes than these, and their determination is even bigger than their biceps."

They watched the ball rocket back and forth on the court.

"You're just making me watch this so I'll stop feeling sorry for myself," Jeremy said.

"Is it working?" his brother asked.

"Absolutely!" Jeremy said. "If those guys can play basketball in wheelchairs, I'm not going to let a broken bone beat me. I can overcome this cast and still have a great summer."

YOUR TURN

1. Can you think of people who have overcome great problems?

_____

PRAYER   God, sometimes it's so easy to give up and feel sorry for myself. Show me how much strength I have and help me become a conqueror. Amen.

ENCOURAGING WORDS

Imagine your friend broke his leg at the beginning of summer. You go to see him and he wants you to write or draw something on his cast. What would you write to make him laugh and feel better?

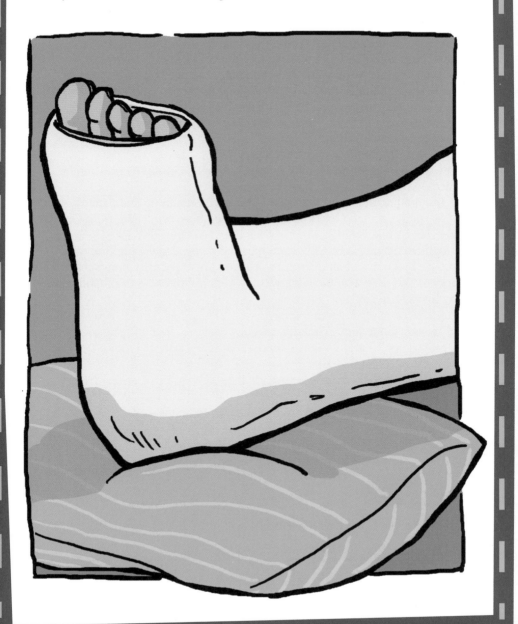

LIFE LESSONS

> **We pass along wisdom and love from one generation to the next.**
> *From generation to generation we will recount your praise.*
> **– Psalm 79:13**

BLACK, WHITE, AND GRAY

"It's time for your chess lesson," Grandpa said. He unfolded the black and white board on the table beside Jeremy's chair and dumped the pieces from the box.

Jeremy chose white and set up his side of the board. He liked the look and feel of the pieces, especially the horse-head knights.

Grandpa shook a finger and said, "Remember the queen goes on her own color."

Jeremy switched positions for the king and queen.

"Today I'm going to teach you how to castle," Grandpa said. He explained the move and let Jeremy try it out.

"You've got it," Grandpa said. "Let's play."

Jeremy moved a pawn forward two spaces. Grandpa brought out a knight.

"How did you learn to play chess, Grandpa?"

"My grandfather taught me," he said. "We lived on a farm, and there wasn't much to do in the winter. Opa, that's what I called him, came here from Germany. He never spoke good English, but he was a fine chess player."

Jeremy liked playing chess, but even more he enjoyed spending time with Grandpa. He had traveled all over the world and knew so many things. He told great stories. The time with Grandpa was a wonderful blessing from God brought about by his broken ankle.

Jeremy moved another pawn forward.

"You're sure about that?" Grandpa asked.

"Uh, maybe not," Jeremy said. He chose a different pawn to move.

"Much better," Grandpa said.

"So you learned chess from your grandfather the way I'm learning from you," Jeremy said.

"I guess it's up to you to teach your grandson," Grandpa said.

Jeremy laughed and said, "That's a long way off."

Grandpa captured a white pawn with his black knight.

"It will be here sooner than you think," he said.

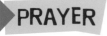
YOUR TURN

1. What things have you learned from people older than you?

_____

▶ PRAYER   God, You have all kinds of ways of giving gifts. Thanks for parents, grandparents, and older people who share their love and learning with me. Amen.

LEARNING ABOUT LIVING

Older people have lived many years and learned a lot of things. That's why we can learn so much from our parents, aunts, uncles, and especially our grandparents. The Bible gives great respect to people who have lived a long time. To learn one thing the Bible says about older people, solve the code below.

You'll need your Bible to solve this puzzle. Fill in each blank with the right letter from the right book of the Bible to break the code. So if the clue says SECOND BOOK, SECOND LETTER, look up the second book of the Bible (Exodus) and fill in the blank with the second letter of that book's name (X). If the code is too hard, you can find the answer at Proverbs 16:31.

FIRST BOOK, FIRST LETTER   _____
EIGHTH BOOK, FIRST LETTER   _____
SIXTH BOOK, LAST LETTER   _____
FIFTH BOOK, LAST LETTER   _____

SIXTEENTH BOOK, LAST LETTER   _____
FIFTEENTH BOOK, LAST LETTER   _____
THIRD BOOK, FOURTH LETTER   _____
FIFTEENTH BOOK, THIRD LETTER   _____

FIRST BOOK, LAST TWO LETTERS   _____

THIRTIETH BOOK, FIRST LETTER   _____

THIRD BOOK, SEVENTH LETTER   _____
EIGHTH BOOK, FIRST LETTER   _____
EIGHTEENTH BOOK, SECOND LETTER   _____
FORTIETH BOOK, LAST LETTER   _____
LAST BOOK, LAST LETTER   _____

■ JESUS JOY ■

God sent Jesus to bring us joy and happiness.

Rejoice in the Lord always. I will say it again: Rejoice!
– Philippians 4:4

WHO KNEW?

Pastor Chris accepted the coffee mug from Jeremy's mother and settled it on his knee. He turned to Jeremy lying on the sofa with his cast.

"I heard you were banged up and I wanted to check on you. Did you really break something or are you just faking it so people will feel sorry for you?" Pastor Chris asked with a sparkle in his eye.

Jeremy said it was a skateboard accident and the minister nodded knowingly.

"When I was about your age I took a spill on my board and ended up with a broken arm," Pastor Chris said.

Jeremy stared in amazement.

"You used to skateboard?" he asked.

"Sure," Pastor Chris said. "Do you think I walked around singing hymns all day when I was a boy?"

"So you were a kid like me?" Jeremy asked.

"Probably crazier than you," Pastor Chris said with a chuckle. "At the hospital, they'd say, 'Here comes Chris again.' Sometime I'll tell you about my tree house and the zip line to my bedroom window. No broken bones, but I got eight stitches."

"What did your parents say?" Jeremy asked.

"My mother threatened to sell me to the gypsies," the minister laughed.

"You're like a regular person," Jeremy said.

"Jeremy, there's no reason Christians can't have fun," Pastor Chris said. "God invented fun, and we're God's kids. Say, do you like to fish?"

"I've never done it," Jeremy said.

"We'll have to fix that," Pastor Chris said. "When you're back on your feet, I'll take the youth group fishing."

"Count me in," Jeremy said. "Who knew spending time with the preacher could be fun?"

YOUR TURN

1. Some people think being a Christian is stuffy and boring. What would you say to someone who thinks this way?

_____

PRAYER God, I'm Your own kid! You love me! That's enough to keep me smiling all day. Amen.

TO BE HAPPY

Have some fun thinking about why Christians are happy. Complete the following sentences.

- God loves me more than

_____.

- Jesus came to save me and that makes me as happy as

_____.

- God gives me friends who stick with me even when I

_____.

- When I am sad, God can pick me up like

_____.

PUTTING IN A GOOD WORD

God wants us to pray for one another.

I urge, then, first of all, that requests, prayers, intercession and thanksgiving be made for everyone.

– I Timothy 2:1

THE LIST

"Jeremy, I need to be on my way," Pastor Chris said. "I have some hospital visits to make this afternoon, but I want to leave this with you."

The minister handed a folded piece of paper to Jeremy.

"What is it?" Jeremy asked. He opened the paper and found a dozen names written on the sheet.

"This week's prayer list," the minister said.

"I don't know these people," Jeremy said.

"You don't have to know them to pray for them," Pastor Chris told him.

"You want me to pray for these people?" Jeremy asked.

"You have time on your hands right now," the minister said, "and every person on that list needs God's help."

Jeremy felt confused and a little scared.

"I don't know how to do that," he admitted.

"Easy as pie," Pastor Chris said. The minister glanced at the paper. "That's Mattie Close at the top of the list. It says she has a broken hip. If you want to pray for Mattie you just talk to God and say, 'Lord, please heal Mattie's hip.'"

"That's all I have to do?"

"Only if you want to," Pastor Chris said. "No pressure."

After Pastor Chris left, Jeremy asked his mother, "Do we have a directory of church members with pictures?"

"Yes, I'll get it for you," she said.

Jeremy leafed through the book and found the photo of Mattie Close. She had white hair and a pleasant smile. He studied the picture.

"God," he said, "please bless Mattie Close and help her get well. Amen."

That wasn't so bad, he thought. It actually felt good.

He pulled out the paper to see who was next on the list.

YOUR TURN

1. Are there people you pray for every day? Do you pray for people who aren't in your family?

God, there are people I care about, and I know You care about them, too. Is it okay if I ask You to take care of them today? Amen.

PRAYER LIST

Make your own list of people to pray for and identify something to prayabout. Complete the list and start praying.

Monday I will pray for _____,
_____.
that God will _____,
Tuesday I will pray for _____,
_____.
that God will _____,
Wednesday I will pray for _____,
_____.
that God will _____,
Thursday I will pray for _____,
_____.
that God will _____,
Friday I will pray for _____,
_____.
that God will _____,
Saturday I will pray for _____,
_____.
that God will _____

MAKING CONTACT

God give us love so we can share it with others.

This is the message you heard from the beginning:
We should love one another.

– I John 3:11

PHONE PHOBIA

"Why don't you call Mrs. Close?" Jeremy asked.

"Is that one of the ladies on your prayer list?" Mom asked.

"She has a broken hip," Jeremy said.

"Why don't you call?" his mother asked.

"I don't even know her," Jeremy said.

"Neither do I," Mom said. "You're the one praying for her."

She pitched the phone to Jeremy as he lay in the reclining chair with his broken ankle propped up.

"What if the phone surprises her and she falls out of bed and breaks her other hip?" Jeremy protested.

Mom raised her eyebrows.

"What if she thinks I'm a pest and calls the police?" Jeremy asked. "How would you like it if I ended up in jail?"

Jeremy picked up the phone and stared at it.

"I'll bet she's deaf and can't even hear the phone," he said.

"I can't believe you are afraid of a sweet old lady. Are you finished talking crazy?" she asked.

"I guess so," Jeremy said. He found her number and called Mrs. Close.

A few minutes later, Jeremy's mother came back.

"How was the phone call?" she asked.

"Mrs. Close is real nice," Jeremy said. "She invited me over for cookies and cocoa. She said I could pray for her hip and she would pray for my ankle."

"No injuries?" Mom asked. "No police on their way to arrest you?"

He studied the prayer list and picked up the phone.

"Don't talk crazy," he said. "I've got more calls to make."

 **YOUR TURN**

1. Is loving somebody just something we feel or does love make us want to help others?

_____

_____

PRAYER   God, I don't want to be so stuck on my own stuff that I forget about others. Show me ways to share Your love today. Amen.

ACTiON PLAN

Everyone has things they're afraid to try or dread doing.
The next time you come up to one of those things, create an action plan.

Task to be done: _____

Start Here

Steps Needed
1.

2.

3.

People Who Might Help

Supplies Needed

Things to Tell Myself to Reduce Fear

What To Do First

What To Do Second

Expected Outcome of My Actions

Have All Steps Completed By This Date

How to Finish Up

LISTENING

> **Being kind to others can make the world better.**
> *Be kind and compassionate to one another.*
> **– Ephesians 4:32**

MEETING IN MATH

"How was therapy today?" Dad asked as Jeremy joined him in the waiting room.

"Lily is a slave driver," Jeremy said. "She's working me really hard, but I'm getting better. I did stuff today I couldn't do last week."

"Who's Lily?" Dad asked, holding the door for his son.

"The therapist," Jeremy said. "She moved here from Florida last year. Her son goes to my school, but I've never met him."

They moved slowly across the parking lot because of Jeremy's walking cast.

"Do Lily and her son like it here?" Dad asked, unlocking the car.

Jeremy settled into the seat and fastened his seat belt.

"Her son misses his old friends," he said. "His grades have tanked, and now he's hanging with some kids Lily doesn't like."

Dad backed the car from the space.

"She's worried," Jeremy said. "She thinks some of these new friends might be into drugs."

"That's bad business," Dad said. "It sounds like both Lily and her son must be having a hard time."

"I guess so. I let Lily look at my class schedule. It turns out that her son and I will be in the same math class," Jeremy said. "I told her I'll introduce him to some of my friends. If he gets with some good kids, maybe it will keep him out of trouble."

"That would be great," his father said. "It's a nice thing for you to do."

They rode along in silence for a while.

"I guess this is one good thing that comes from therapy," Jeremy said. "Wouldn't it be cool if God used my busted ankle to help Lily's son?"

"Yes," Dad said. "Super cool."

YOUR TURN

1. Do you think listening to someone with problems might make that person feel better? Does it help you to have someone listen?

 **PRAYER**

God, everybody has problems, not just me. Sometimes when I help others, my problems don't seem so big. Amen.

GOOD LISTENER?

Are you a good listener? Put a star next to the things you want people to do when you are talking, and put an X over the things you don't want people to do when you are talking. Then, circle the things you need to work on to be a better listener for others.

■ MAKING A DIFFERENCE ■

Following Jesus means offering our lives to him.

Whoever serves me must follow me.
– John 12:26

WHEN I GROW UP

Jeremy studied the chess board.

"Aren't you ever going to let me win?" Jeremy asked his Grandpa.

"Nope," Grandpa said. "When you beat me, you'll know it was all you."

Grandpa captured Jeremy's rook with his bishop.

"Keep your eyes open," Grandpa said.

Jeremy felt his mind wander from the game.

"I might like to be a physical therapist when I grow up," Jeremy said.

"Yes?" Grandpa said, raising his eye from the chess board. "Tell me more."

"Physical therapists help people get better after accidents and surgery," Jeremy said. "They exercise people and give massages and stuff. I might like making people healthier."

"You're good with people," Grandpa said. "You would do well in work like that. Physical therapy is a job that makes the world better."

"I think so," Jeremy agreed.

"Making money is fine," Grandpa said, "but you want work worth doing. Let God help you decide. Some people only pick a job because of what it pays or because it's not too hard. But if we're going to follow Jesus," he sat back in his chair, "we follow him at work, too."

"If I hadn't broken my ankle," Jeremy said, "I wouldn't even know there was such a thing as physical therapy."

"It takes a lot of school to become a physical therapist," Grandpa said.

Jeremy moved his queen to protect his other rook.

"I could do it," Jeremy said. "I get good grades when I'm studying something I care about."

"You can do anything you really want to do," Grandpa said. He moved his own queen and said, "Checkmate."

"Except beat you at chess," Jeremy said.

"One of these days," Grandpa said.

1. Have you thought about what work you might do someday? How will you make up your mind about a job?

PRAYER — God, it's scary trying to figure out what I might do when I grow up. Please help me find the right work. Amen.

WHEEL OF CAREERS

Y ou can't think about becoming something you don't even know about. Use this exercise to find out about some new careers. Ask three people what kinds of work they do. (Try to ask people for whom you don't already know their careers.) Then ask them to tell you why this is a good job for them. Record their answers on this career wheel below.

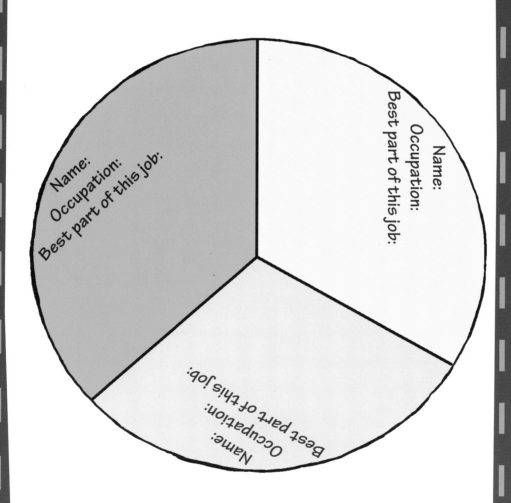

TURNING OFF THE TELEVISION

Learning is a gift from God to help us grow.

Let the wise listen and add to their learning.

– Proverbs 1:5

MAD DOGS AND SPOOKY GUYS

Jeremy's ankle was hurting and he shifted the heavy cast, trying to get more comfortable. He was clicking through television stations when his mother laid three library books on the table at his side.

"What's this?" Jeremy asked.

"I called the school to find out what you'll be reading in English this fall," she said. "You can get a head start."

"You expect me to spend my summer vacation reading stupid school books?" Jeremy complained.

"They're not stupid," his mother said. She picked up one of the books and looked at it fondly. "I read *To Kill a Mockingbird* when I was your age, and I loved it."

Jeremy returned to surfing channels and ignored the books.

His mother said, "You don't have to read them, but I'll leave them in case you get bored."

Jeremy turned off the television and muttered, "Daytime TV is the worst."

He stared out the window for a while. Idly, he picked up the top book from the stack and leafed through it. There was some kid named Scout in the book, kind of a cool name. He found a chapter where a man had to shoot a mad dog. That was different.

With nothing better to do, he flipped back to the first page and began to read. When his mother brought his lunch on a tray, he was twenty-five pages into the book.

"What about the creepy guy in the old house?" Jeremy asked. "Is he a bad guy or does he care about the main characters?"

"Keep reading and you'll find out," his mother said.

"I didn't know reading could be so much fun," Jeremy said. "This might be the year I get an "A" in English."

His mother just smiled.

YOUR TURN

1. Why aren't we born knowing everything we need to know?

_____

PRAYER God, Your world is filled with awesome things. The more I learn, the more I see what an amazing world You've made. Amen.

I'M LEARNING AND GROWING

Sometimes we don't realize how much we are learning and growing. Complete the chart about the things you've learned and then thank God for all these things and for the people who help you.

1. Things I learned in school last year

_____

2. Things I've learned to do at home that help our family

_____

3. Things I've learned in church

_____

4. Things I've learned about myself

_____

5. Things I've learned to make or operate

_____

4 feet TALL

Learned to Ride a Bike

Got a puppy!

5th Birthday

PASS THE POPCORN

Life is better when we spend time with people we love.

Be devoted to one another in brotherly love.
– Romans 12:10

BLAZING SIX GUNS

"My turn to pick the movie," Jeremy's father said as they finished dinner.

"A cowboy movie?" Mom guessed.

"Blazing Six Guns," Dad said. "Outlaws, bounty hunters—this has it all."

"Ooh, I can hardly wait," Mom said. "I'll make the popcorn.

"While I clear the table and load the dishwasher," Dad said.

"And I'll set up the movie," Jeremy's brother Reese volunteered.

Jeremy got up from the table. Thanks to his broken ankle, he was released from kitchen chores. He hobbled into the living room.

"Wednesday night family movies," Jeremy said. "It's really corny."

His brother Reese opened the movie case and took out the DVD. He rubbed a smudge from the shiny surface.

"Mom and Dad are doing this to keep you company," Reese said.

"Don't tell them I said so," Jeremy admitted, "but I think it's fun."

"Dad always picks goofy westerns and Mom does chick flicks," Reese said.

"Even if the movie is lame," Jeremy said, "at least we're spending time together. That's the part I like."

"And the popcorn," Reese said. "Parmesan popcorn at that!"

"Remember the night Dad made Cajun corn and sprinkled red pepper over the cheese," Jeremy said.

"My tongue hasn't stopped burning yet," Reese said.

They both laughed. A few minutes later Jeremy's parents joined them, his mother carrying a heaping bowl of popcorn.

"When my ankle heals," Jeremy asked, "will we keep doing movie nights?"

"Would you like to?" Dad asked.

"Sure, it would be okay," Jeremy said.

His mother leaned over and hugged him.

"It would be okay with me, too," she said. "Have some popcorn."

YOUR TURN

1. What fun things do you enjoy with your family?

_____

PRAYER   God, my family isn't perfect and sometimes we fight, but I love them and I like to have fun with them. So thanks for giving me my family. I'm glad I'm not alone. Amen.

A BUDDY

Lots of things are more fun when we do them with friends. Draw pictures of the people who might share these things with you.

Play Games

Watch A Movie

Eat A Pizza

See A Ballgame

Do Homework

Rake Leaves

SAVING THE PIECES

God is always at work bringing good things from bad things.

And we know that in all things God works for the good of those who love him, who have been called according to his purpose.
– Romans 8:28

THE GREATEST SUMMER

The doctor turned off the saw and pulled away Jeremy's cast in two pieces. The skin underneath was shiny and pink.

"Yucchh!" Jeremy said. "That stinks!"

"Soap and water will take care of the smell," the doctor said. He turned Jeremy's foot, examining his ankle. "The bone has healed very well."

"Just in time," Jeremy said. "I'm glad to get out of that cast before school starts next week."

"Not much of a summer vacation," the doctor said. "All those weeks laid up in a cast."

"Can I keep the cast?" Jeremy asked.

"Why would you want to?" the doctor asked.

"To remind me of a great summer," Jeremy said. "I learned to play chess and spent bunches of time with my grandpa. We had family movie night every week with parmesan popcorn. I got to know my preacher, and he showed me how to pray for sick people. Now some of those sick people are my friends. I found out about physical therapy, and I think that might be my job someday. I read some great books. And when school starts next week, I'm going to meet my therapist's son, he seems like a cool guy."

The doctor's eyes widened.

"Are you telling me the broken ankle was a good thing?" he asked.

"No, a broken bone is a bad thing," Jeremy said. "But God used it to bless me."

"Good things came from a bad thing," the doctor said.

"Yes," Jeremy said. "God can take the crummiest stuff and use it for something really great!"

The doctor smiled broadly and squeezed Jeremy's shoulder.

"You've learned a lot this summer," he said. "I wish all of my patients were as smart as you."

YOUR TURN

1. Can you think of a bad thing in your life that led to good things?

_____

PRAYER — God, when Jesus went to the cross, You took the worst thing of all and used it to save the world. I trust You to use the bad things in my life for something good. Amen.

FROM NEGATIVE TO POSITIVE

God can help you change the negative or unfortunate things that happen into positive experiences. To help you remember God's promise, unscramble the words below and match the negative feelings on the left to the good things on the right.

GREAN   STRUT

SNADSSE   SNIROGVEFSE

RAEF   LIHNEAG

TRUH   YOJ

ANSWER KEY

CHAPTER 1

THE CREATOR   page 9

On the first day, God made LIGHT. And it was good.

On the second day, God made the SKY. And it was amazing.

On the third day, God made the LAND and the SEA. And it was terrific.

On the fourth day, God made the SUN, MOON, and STARS. And it was great.

On the fifth day, God made FISHES and BIRDS. And it was wonderful.

On the sixth day, God made DOGS, CATS, and all kinds of animals. God also made PEOPLE. And it was totally awesome.

On the seventh day, God RESTED.

HERE, THERE, AND EVERYWHERE!   page 11

God is with me...

in the darkest CAVE

above the CLOUDS

if I fly to the MOON

in a TREE

in the WILDERNESS

on a MOUNTAIN

on the SEA

WHAT A HELPER! page 13

```
S  P  G  N  I  L  A  E  H  U  I  E
C  A  R  Q  E  D  S  H  F  P  O  G
O  M  R  J  T  U  E  H  N  Q  W  J
U  M  P  J  C  O  M  F  O  R  T  I
R  W  A  Q  P  S  I  T  I  S  L  Y
A  D  T  H  G  D  W  P  T  N  M  L
G  U  I  D  A  N  C  E  C  O  F  I
E  M  E  B  A  E  E  A  E  Y  E  M
N  D  N  V  I  I  J  C  T  V  D  A
L  F  C  K  F  R  U  E  O  S  A  F
D  H  E  I  E  F  W  L  R  P  D  I
B  X  Z  H  G  D  P  F  P  W  T  A
```

IMMUTABLE page 17

YOU REMAIN THE SAME, AND YOUR YEARS WILL NEVER END.

GOD ONLY KNOWS page 19

Things that FRIGHTEN you

Things that make you HAPPY

Your GOALS

Your SUCCESSES

Your SECRETS

How many HAIRS ARE ON YOUR HEAD

PRACTICING PATIENCE page 21

BE PATIENT WITH EVERYONE.

GOD IS LOVE, SO IS JESUS
page 29

Jesus gave sight to the BLIND

Jesus fed the HUNGRY

Jesus healed the SICK

Jesus forgave SINNERS

Jesus made friends with the LONELY

Jesus played with CHILDREN

Jesus brought the dead back to LIFE

Jesus loved EVERYBODY

CHAPTER 2

STAND BACK, SPIDER-MAN!
page 35
ABISHAI
BENAIAH
SHAMGAR
SAMSON
GIDEON
STEPHEN

VOICE MAIL page 43
God Says: CALL ME AND I WILL ANSWER.

JUST ASK! page 45
Ask and it will be given to you; seek and you will find; knock and the door will be opened to you. For everyone who asks receives; he who seeks finds; and to him who knocks, the door will be opened. Which of you, if his son asks for bread, will give him a stone? Or if he asks for a fish, will give him a snake? If you, then, though you are evil, know how to give good gifts to your children, how much more will your Father in heaven give good gifts to those who ask him!

LEARNING THE LIBRARY
page 51

Old Testament

LAW
* Genesis
* Exodus
* Leviticus
* Numbers
* Deuteronomy

HISTORY
* Joshua
* Judges
* Ruth
* 1 Samuel
* 2 Samuel
* 1 Kings
* 2 Kings
* 1 Chronicles
* 2 Chronicles
* Ezra
* Nehemiah
* Esther

WISDOM AND POETRY
* Job
* Psalms
* Proverbs
* Ecclesiastes
* Song of Solomon

MAJOR PROPHETS

* Isaiah

* Jeremiah

* Lamentations

* Ezekiel

* Daniel

MINOR PROPHETS

* Hosea

* Joel

* Amos

* Obadiah

* Jonah

* Micah

* Nahum

* Habakkuk

* Zephaniah

* Haggai

* Zechariah

* Malachi

New Testament

GOSPELS

* Matthew

* Mark

* Luke

* John

CHURCH HISTORY

* Acts

PAUL'S LETTERS

* Romans

* 1 Corinthians

* 2 Corinthians

* Galatians

* Ephesians

* Philippians

* Colossians

* 1 Thessalonians

* 2 Thessalonians

* 1 Timothy

* 2 Timothy

* Titus

* Philemon

OTHER LETTERS

* Hebrews

* James

* 1 Peter

* 2 Peter

* 1 John

* 2 John

* 3 John

* Jude

VISIONS

* Revelation

CHAPTER 3

SAFE AND SOUND   page 69

HE WILL COVER YOU WITH
HIS FEATHERS. (Psalm 91:4)

WHY RULES? page 75

Chapter 4

BREAKING FREE page 81
RESPECT, TRUTH, PLANNING

NOT JUST FOR GROWN-UPS
page 93

Don't let anyone look down on you because you are YOUNG, but set an example for the believers in SPEECH, in LIFE, in LOVE, in FAITH and in PURITY.
I Timothy 4:12

KEEPING ANGER UNDER CONTROL page 105

Chapter 5

CAUTION: GOD AT WORK
page 113

ENCIRCLED BY LOVE page 117
GOD IS ALWAYS BIGGER THAN OUR PROBLEMS!

ON A STORMY DAY page 119

One day, Jesus and his friends were on a BOAT when a terrible STORM began. Their BOAT started to SINK. Jesus didn't worry because he was SLEEPING. His friends were SCARED and begged Jesus to SAVE them. Jesus got up and told the STORM to STOP. When the danger passed, the disciples were GRATEFUL because Jesus saved them. Jesus said to them, "Where is your FAITH?"

HOW HEALTHY ARE YOU?

page 121

TWO THINGS   page 127

ANYTHING and EVERYTHING

CHAPTER 6

WE DON'T HAVE TO WORRY
page 135

Jesus Christ is the same YESTERDAY and TODAY and FOREVER.

WHAT DOES LOVE LOOK LIKE?   page 137

Love the Lord your...

Wheel 1: God with all your heart and soul and mind

Wheel 2: and love your neighbor as yourself.

EASTER SURPRISE   page 141

CHAPTER 7

COAT = LOVE page 177

KIDS NEED CARE page 181

CHAPTER 8

WORKING TOGETHER page 187
PUTTING OUR GIFTS TO WORK page 189
FOR WE ARE GOD'S FELLOW WORKERS.

MAKING YOUR OWN HONEY SANDWICH page 195
WHATEVER IS TRUE,
WHATEVER IS NOBLE,
WHATEVER IS RIGHT,
WHATEVER IS PURE,
WHATEVER IS LOVELY,
WHATEVER IS ADMIRABLE,
THINK ABOUT SUCH THINGS.

FOLLOWING JESUS page 197

KEEPING WATCH page 199
NOAH – Genesis 8:1
DANIEL – Daniel 6:16
DAVID – 1 Kings 17:44-45
SAMSON – Judges 14:5-6
PAUL – Acts 16:22-26

FANTASTIC FEET page 201
I have claws that give me traction for fast running. (CHEETAH)

I have feet that can taste flowers. (BUTTERFLY)

I have feet that let me walk on the ceiling. (GECKO LIZARD)

I have locking feet so I can sleep on a branch without falling. (ROBIN)

My flat feet help me swim. (DUCK)

I have hundreds of feet for creeping everywhere. (MILLIPEDE)

I use my clawed feet to dig under the earth. (MOLE)

NO BUSY SIGNAL page 203
THE EYES OF THE LORD WATCH OVER THOSE WHO DO RIGHT AND HIS EARS ARE OPEN TO THEIR PRAYERS.

CHAPTER 9